Pelican Books

Anxiety and Neuro

Charles Rycroft was born in 1914 and educated at
Wellington College and Trinity College, Cambridge,
where he took an honours degree in economics
and was a research student in modern history. He
took his M.B. at University College Hospital and
worked as house physician in psychiatry at the
Maudsley Hospital. He has had a private practice as a
psycho-analyst since 1947, and from 1956 to 1968
he was a part-time Consultant in Psychotherapy at
the Tavistock Clinic. He has reviewed for *The Times
Literary Supplement*, the *Observer*, *New Society*, the
New York Review of Books and the *New Statesman*. His
publications include *A Critical Dictionary of Psychoanalysis*
(published in Penguins), *Imagination and Reality*, a
collection of papers originally written for learned
journals, and *Reich*. He was contributing editor of
Psychoanalysis Observed (published as a Pelican in 1968),
and also contributed to *The God I Want* and *Symbols and
Sentiments*.

Anxiety and Neurosis

Charles Rycroft

Foreword by G. M. Carstairs

Penguin Books

Penguin Books Ltd, Harmondsworth,
Middlesex, England
Penguin Books, 625 Madison Avenue,
New York, New York 10022, U.S.A.
Penguin Books Australia Ltd, Ringwood,
Victoria, Australia
Penguin Books Canada Ltd, 2801 John Street,
Markham, Ontario, Canada L3R 1B4
Penguin Books (N.Z.) Ltd, 182–190 Wairau Road,
Auckland 10, New Zealand

First published by Allen Lane The Penguin Press 1968
Published in Pelican Books 1970
Reprinted 1971, 1973, 1976, 1978

Made and printed in Great Britain by
Cox & Wyman Ltd,
London, Reading and Fakenham
Set in Monotype Garamond

Contents

Foreword

One reason for the violent opposition which greeted the early publications of Freud and his fellow psycho-analysts was that they held up a mirror before the human psyche, and the image there presented was an unflattering one. Mankind's collective self-esteem had only recently taken a hard knock, when Darwin shattered the age-old belief that we were made in God's image and were set apart from all the rest of the animal creation. At least, our grandfathers consoled themselves, *homo sapiens* is a *rational* being – and then Freud demonstrated how precarious, and how fitful, is our rationality.

During the course of the twentieth century we have found it progressively easier (helped no doubt by world events of monumental irrationality) to concede that we are all too often swayed by emotion rather than by reason, and for the most part by emotions of which we ourselves are only imperfectly aware. As a result, we have come to recognize that the symptoms of neurotically ill patients are only an exaggeration of experiences common to us all, and hence that the unravelling of the psycho-dynamics of neurosis can teach us more about ourselves.

The desire for self-knowledge has undoubtedly attracted many of the general public to study works of popularization by psycho-analysts; but critical readers, and especially those trained in scientific disciplines, have at times been put off by the analysts' esoteric terminology and by their implicit assumption that psycho-dynamic explanations need not conform to the requirements of every scientific discipline; namely, that hypotheses should be subjected to the test of experiment or controlled observation.

Not all psycho-analysts deserve these strictures: there are, for example, several groups of analytically-oriented research workers both in Britain and the U.S.A. who have adapted the concepts and methods of observation of ethology to test their ideas about particular aspects of human behaviour. The author of this book, although a psycho-analyst of high repute, makes it refreshingly plain that he regards himself primarily as a biologist, addressing himself to the understanding of those recurring, maladaptive behaviour-patterns which we term neurotic. He points out that anxiety, like the sensation of pain, is an experience which helps us to cope not only with external dangers, but also with threats which come from within. The experience of 'helpful anxiety' is common to us all: it enables athletes and actors to produce their best performances and acts as a spur in our efforts to overcome the difficulties we encounter in everyday living. Dr Rycroft argues that in biological terms anxiety consists of a heightened state of vigilance, stimulated by the awareness of threat to one's safety – or to one's peace of mind. When an animal feels threatened, it responds in three basic ways, by attack, or flight or submission. Parallels to these three modes of response can be seen in the three principal defences against anxiety which are represented in neurotic behaviour: the obsessional defence, which counter-attacks by controlling the subject's own feelings, and tries to control other people as well; the phobic reactions, in which one takes flight from the anxiety-provoking situation; the schizoid, like the phobic person, finds the world full of threats but unlike the phobic he cannot easily escape into a place of safety because his fears of the external world remain unallayed, so that his only resource is to deny reality and take refuge in fantasy.

Hysteria, which loomed so large in Freud's private practice, can be seen as another form of the submissive response to threat: in Rycroft's view, it is engendered by parental attitudes which make the young child feel defeated, inferior and unloveable, so that she does not dare to assert herself openly, but only through guile. Hysterical symptoms are extremely susceptible to changes in popular concepts of what is acceptable in the 'sick role'. Nowadays gross conversion symptoms are out of fashion, having been replaced by displays of extreme spinelessness and dependency on the part of both men and women patients.

The author is agreeably undoctrinaire in his appraisal of the differing points of view of rival schools of psychoanalysis, and those of the behaviour-therapists. He indicates that what they all have in common, in the treatment situation, is the cooperation of patient and therapist in a shared undertaking. He is atypical, also, in recognizing the value of supportive psychotherapy, that age-old means of helping one another by lending a sympathetic ear, by permitting a temporary emotional dependency and by offering sympathy and maybe even a modicum of advice. This simple transaction goes on thousands of times in every community, and can often be carried out quite adequately (and much more economically) by counsellors drawn from many walks of life, rather than by highly trained professionals. It seems very likely that the need for both simple counselling and for more expert forms of insight-giving psychotherapy will increase in modern society. Dr Rycroft's book gives hope that by returning to biological principles, students of human behaviour may be able to base our future therapies on a more secure scientific foundation.

G. M. CARSTAIRS

Introduction

A young woman was so anxious whenever she left home that she was unable to do so unaccompanied; and yet when a car in which she was a passenger was involved in an accident, she kept her head, gave first aid and called for the police without hesitation. A laboratory assistant, one of whose regular duties was to take samples of blood from experimental animals, became anxious and nearly fainted, as he watched a sample of his own blood being taken by a doctor. Another man seemed entirely at ease as the doctor he had consulted took his history but started trembling like a leaf when he was asked to lie on the examination couch.

There is something peculiar about these three incidents. Why should a woman who can deal competently with an emergency be terrified at the prospect of walking out of her front door? Why should a man who takes blood from animals daily be upset by being on the receiving end of a procedure he knows well? And why should a man who trusts his doctor enough to visit him and talk freely to him be alarmed at the prospect of being examined by him? In each case an intense and distressing emotional reaction has been evoked by a situation which seems inappropriate and inadequate to cause it.

There is, however, nothing peculiar about the emotional

reactions in themselves. If the young woman's home had been a dug-out and her street a battlefield, her anxiety would seem entirely natural. We can all imagine ourselves being suddenly confronted by some sight so ghastly that we nearly faint. If the doctor's examination couch had been a torture-chamber, we would have expected his patient to tremble like a leaf. And if they had been children and not adults, their anxiety would not strike us as surprising. Clearly in each case some factor which does not belong to the realities of the situation is in operation, and it has compelled these three persons to behave out of character and to react as though they were confronted with a situation other than the one that they were, and knew they were, in.

Anxiety of this kind, which is provoked by situations which appear to give no grounds for it and which seems as absurd and irrational to the person experiencing it as it does to others, is known as neurotic anxiety. The purpose of this book is to give some account of anxiety, of its biological origin and function, of its relation to other unpleasant emotions, and of those illnesses, the neuroses, of which it is a major symptom.

One of my aims in writing it has been to do something to dispel the idea, now widely current, that *all* anxiety is irrational, abnormal and neurotic and to show that, on the contrary, the capacity to be anxious is a biological function necessary for survival. I have, therefore, begun by giving an account of the relation of anxiety, as experienced by both healthy and neurotic individuals, to the phenomenon known to physiologists as vigilance, i.e. the capacity to alert oneself immediately to unexpected and unexplained changes in the environment. I have then gone on to describe how the fact that human beings internalize their environment and tend to become alienated from aspects of their own nature, leads to the development of a specifically human type of vigilance, anxiety provoked by internal psychological threats to the integrity of the conscious personality. I have then tried to show that the neuroses can be understood as disturbances in the capacity to master anxiety and, furthermore, that the various types of neurosis can be understood as the effects of defensive manoeuvres analogous to those used by animals in objectively dangerous situations. I have ended by giving a descriptive account of the neuroses and of the forms of treatment at present available.

Throughout I have been concerned to do two things: to show that neurotic behaviour can be understood imaginatively as being the result of conflicts that to a greater or lesser extent are present in us all; and to maintain the unity of science by demonstrating the extent to which human psychopathology can be shown to exemplify well-known biological principles.

Chapter 1

Anxiety, Fear and Expectancy

Anxiety is such a common experience that one would be disinclined to believe anyone who claimed to be immune to it, but its precise nature and function are by no means self-evident. Is it a symptom of neurosis which would never occur in a person who enjoyed perfect mental health, or has it a positive function? What indeed do we mean when we say that someone is anxious, to what sort of experience or experiences are we referring? If someone says that he feels anxious in crowds, or that he is anxious about his wife's health, or that he is anxious to see some particular film, to what emotion is he referring? Is there indeed anything in common between these three usages of the word?

ANXIETY AND APPREHENSIVENESS

In the first instance, when someone says that crowds – or heights or spiders – make him anxious, there can, I think, be little doubt but that he wishes to convey two things: first, that he feels apprehensive in crowds, tries to avoid them, and, if he ever is in one, wishes to escape; and secondly, that he senses or suspects that his apprehensiveness is inappropriate and that something other and more than the realistic danger of, perhaps, being crushed or assaulted, is responsible for it. Or alternatively, if he does maintain that his fear is justified, he will do so defensively, knowing that he is running in the face of the conviction of others that his fear is exaggerated or imaginary. In this case anxiety is a form of fear or apprehensiveness which has been evoked by an inappropriate or inadequate stimulus and which, it must therefore be inferred, is really due to some psychological factor or complex which he does not himself understand. It must also be inferred that crowds, or heights or spiders, have acquired a private, unconscious symbolic meaning, as a result of which being in a crowd means something different to him than it does to someone who feels at ease in one.

Anxiety of this kind is, in principle at least, a symptom, even though it may occur so infrequently and may appear so trivial that it would be absurd to suggest that everyone who has ever experienced it should seek psychiatric treatment. Irrational fears of this kind are indeed almost universal in childhood and most adults will admit to having dislikes and distastes which they cannot justify rationally. In some people, however, anxiety of this kind occurs so frequently and with such intensity as to be almost totally incapacitating, and it is one of the commonest presenting symptoms of those who do seek psychiatric treatment. The situations or objects which provoke such anxiety are legion, but perhaps the most frequent are open or enclosed spaces, travelling, snakes, spiders, heights and thunder. In psychiatric terminology these fears are known as phobias. Psycho-analytical investigation shows regularly that the phobic object or situation has become a symbol for some aspect of the patient himself and that his anxiety really refers to his dread of being confronted with some repressed part of himself.

If all instances of anxiety were of this kind it would be possible to define anxiety as irrational fear and proceed without further ado to the psychopathology of anxiety. But, as I hope to show, there is really more to the problem of anxiety than this.

ANXIETY AND CONCERN

If we turn now to the case of someone saying that he is anxious about his wife's health, it is again, I think, clear that he wishes to convey two things: first, that he is concerned about his wife's health and wishes to do something about it; and second, that there is to his mind something uncertain about either the nature or the outcome of her illness. If we analyse the emotion of concern we find that it resembles apprehensiveness in including fear but differs from it in that the fear is not, directly at least, on one's own behalf but on behalf of someone one cares for. Concern also evokes a wish to take action though the action in this case is not removal of oneself from the situation which makes one apprehensive but alteration of the circumstances that are causing the concern. Anxious concern also resembles apprehensiveness in containing an unknown or undisclosed element but differs from it in that this is not the intrusion of irrational psychological factors but the uncertainty that exists as to what is really the matter and how serious it is. Anxious concern then resembles apprehensiveness in three ways – it includes an element of fear, it provokes a wish to take action and it contains an uncertain element – but differs from it in two others; it is experienced on behalf of another and not of oneself, and the type of action it tends to evoke is not avoidance but alteration of the situation. These differences, however, are not differences in the emotion itself but in the circumstances arousing it and it would indeed be possible to define anxiety and concern in terms of one another, anxiety being concern on one's own behalf and concern being anxiety on another's behalf, the apparent difference between the two being really dependent on a largely artificial distinction between the interests of oneself and those one cares for. If one thinks of the way in which many mothers worry about their children's health – and many men about their car or their garden – one realizes that it is often impossible to distinguish between anxiety about oneself and concern for others.

For the sake of simplicity I have so far treated apprehensive anxiety about oneself as though it were always unjustified and anxious concern as though it were always justified. This is, of course, not so, and just as the anxious person may have real grounds for, say, fearing that he will lose his job, so the concerned person may be unnecessarily anxious. Hence the term 'over-anxious' which is used to make the distinction between anxious concern which is appropriate and that which is due to some undisclosed psychological factor. Doctors are as familiar with over-anxious parents and relatives as they are with anxious patients and those who work in Children's Departments and Child Guidance Clinics are often impressed by the frequency with which they have to shift their attention from the child, whose symptoms are the apparent problem, to the over-anxiety of its parents; and many a solicitous mother has at first been indignant, and then later relieved, to discover that the doctor is treating her and not her child as the patient. The over-anxious concern of neurotic parents is in a sense false concern since it is personal apprehensiveness masquerading as concern for others and is an indication not of devotion towards their children but of ambivalence towards them and towards their own parental role.

ANXIETY AND ALERTNESS

The two forms of anxiety that I have already discussed – apprehensiveness and anxious concern – are obviously forms of fear. But what of the person who says that he is anxious to see some particular film? Is he just speaking loosely, or is he using the word in a way that reveals another aspect of the problem of anxiety? This question is not a trivial one, since, as I shall describe later, there have been psychologists who have explicitly rejected the idea that anxiety has anything whatsoever to do with fear. Someone who says that he is anxious to go to a film is clearly not frightened at the prospect of going into a cinema and one is indeed tempted to think that he has used the word 'anxious' when a more precise or pedantic person would have said 'keen' or 'eager'. But this would, I think, be wrong, since he is also saying, or at least implying, that he is prepared to exert himself to see the film and that he is alive to the possibility of his having to overcome obstacles to his doing so. The feature common to this eager sort of anxiety and to apprehensiveness and concern is not fear but a state of alertness or preparedness to perform some action, the precise nature of which is as yet uncertain. He will have to find out when and where the film is showing and make sure that he has an evening free from other engagements.

That anxiety is essentially a matter of alertness or watchfulness was the view taken by Shand and McDougall, two of the psychologists who rejected the idea that anxiety is a form of fear. According to them anxiety is not a simple, primary emotion like fear but a complex emotion or mood, which forms the second member of the series hope, anxiety, despondency and despair. These emotions resemble one another in indicating the individual's attitude towards his wish to achieve or acquire something, but they differ in respect of the assessment of the likelihood of the wish being fulfilled; the hopeful person anticipates that it will and does not expect to encounter any serious difficulties; the anxious person expects to encounter difficulties and believes that he will have to make a special effort if he is to overcome them; the despondent person is overwhelmed by the anticipated difficulties but still thinks that there is an off-chance of achieving his ends, while the hopeless person thinks that it is useless to try. On this view, the presence of hope, anxiety, despondency or despair depends on an intellectual assessment of the nature and extent of the obstacles interposed between the self and his ends, even though this assessment is not necessarily accurate since it may be influenced by his temperament; and a person may start by being hopeful, then encounter an obstacle which makes him anxious, and then become despondent or despairing if the difficulties begin to appear insuperable.

If Shand and McDougall are right in supposing that the essence of anxiety is the state of watchfulness evoked by recognition of the fact that action is necessary if a wish is to be fulfilled, anxiety is certainly not intrinsically a symptom – even though particular instances of it may be – and it is not an emotion which a person enjoying perfect mental health would be immune to. On the contrary it performs the necessary function of alerting the individual so that he is enabled to perceive and overcome obstacles which lie in his path and without which he would be either blindly optimistic or helplessly pessimistic.

The value of anxiety as a means of mobilizing energy to overcome obstacles is well illustrated by the following quotation from *The Daily Mail* (20 February 1965)

Steak-and-nerves · *By Brian James*

Chelsea have ordered steaks for breakfast to begin the day in which they must meet and master Tottenham in the F.A. Cup. But manager Tom Docherty will be delighted if some are pushed away uneaten.

'Before one of our biggest games several of my players were physically sick. They were tense, nervous. And that's the way I want them tomorrow,' he said last night.

'Great football comes from players who are anxious and keyed up. This has been a week in which Chelsea have been heaped with praise.

'Now for me the greatest danger to us today is complacency. On the morning of a match like this I'd rather have them sick than smiling.

'I'll look along the tables tomorrow. If they look too settled, too much as though they are taking this great game in their stride, it will be up to me to make it clear what they face.

'I know all about Spurs' record away. It does not mean a thing. They have great players. Greaves can ghost past three men and destroy you in a flash. Only an alert and anxious team can stop him.'

ANXIETY AND THE FUTURE

Shand and McDougall's view of anxiety highlights an aspect of anxiety which is not immediately obvious if one approaches it from the angle of pathology with its inevitable preoccupation with the painful and irrational. This is the fact that anxiety is an emotion concerned with the future. An anxious person is not anxious about what has happened, nor even about what is happening, but about what may happen. (The few apparent exceptions derive from the fact that one can be anxious about what one will discover has already happened.) Since the future is always uncertain an element of anxiety enters into our attitude towards it, notwithstanding our attempts to reduce anxiety by plans for personal and social security or by reliance on ideologies such as science and religion which give us the illusion that the future is either predictable or will at least continue to conform to a familiar and comprehensible pattern. Neurotic anxiety is also about the future. The neurotic who is anxious in crowds or is frightened of heights is not frightened of his present experience of being in a crowded tube train or of being on the top of a cliff but of what he imagines might happen. He is fearful lest the cliff crumble or he be overcome by a compulsion to jump off it, lest he be crushed by the crowd or be compelled to kick his fellow-passengers. In every case the distress is not about the present situation but about some imagined possible event in the immediate future. Since phobic people are usually not conscious of what this future event is, their anxiety is not, strictly speaking, a fear of, say, heights, but dread of the unknown which occurs when they

7

are on a height. Since this dreaded event never in fact occurs no amount of standing on cliffs or travelling in crowded trains will cure the anxiety by converting dread of the unknown future into a confrontation with the present.

Similarly, anxious concern relates to some possible but as yet unclearly defined disaster that may befall the object of one's concern and not to his present distress. Certain bad news gives relief from anxiety as effectively as good news since, as I shall explain in a later chapter, anxiety is incompatible with sorrow and grief.

Since anxiety is directed towards the future only those who feel that they have a future are ever anxious and, conversely, being anxious is an indication that one is not entirely without hope for the future. No one who is really convinced that he will fail an examination is ever anxious about it. Some neurotics know how to reverse the relationship between anxiety and despair and succeed in persuading themselves that they are in despair in order to avoid feeling anxious and will, for instance, scratch from an examination in order to avoid the anxiety of taking it and waiting for the results. Those who genuinely suffer from a sense of futility are also conspicuously free of anxiety and one of the most startling poems of despair ever written in English, James Thomson's 'The City of Dreadful Night' has as its refrain 'No hope could have no fear'. This is presumably an echo of Spinoza's 'Fear cannot be without hope, nor hope without fear'.

Anxiety, then, is a sign of life and one is tempted to say that, like hope, it springs eternal in the human breast. Its relation to alertness and to the physical consequences of alertness – the raised muscle tone, the faster and stronger pulse, the heightening of perception – is responsible for the fact that there can be something pleasurable and invigorating about being anxious. Although it is, of course, recognized that some of the thrill of dangerous sports derives from the fact that they arouse fear, victims of neurotic anxiety and concern only rarely admit that they in any way enjoy it – even though it may on occasion be obvious to their friends and relatives. In both instances there is, of course, a quantitative factor involved. Both objectively justified fear and neurotic anxiety may be pleasurable so long as it is not too intense and so long as one feels master of the situation. As soon, however, as one loses control of the situation, the sense of impending disaster obliterates the pleasure. Libidinization of anxiety, in the sense that anxiety has become a substitute for all other kinds of pleasure, is usually totally unconscious and only occurs in people who have lost contact with all other sources of liveliness and pleasure.

SIGNAL-ANXIETY

If Shand and McDougall are right in supposing that anxiety has the general biological function of preparing the individual for action, then apprehensiveness and concern are two special instances of its operation which have in common the fact that they are aroused by the expectation of danger and not of opportunity, and that they are capable of exaggeration by unconscious psychological factors. It is this latter fact which is responsible for the contemporary tendency, not only of psychiatrists but also of the general public, to think of anxiety as a neurotic symptom.

Although this tendency to think of anxiety as an irrational form of fear is largely due to the influence of psycho-analysis, Freud's later theory of anxiety, which he expounded in his *Inhibitions, Symptoms and Anxiety*, in fact resembles McDougall's in many respects. In this book Freud discarded his original view that anxiety is a way of discharging repressed libido and replaced it by a distinction between two different kinds of anxiety, neither of which is libidinal. One he called primary anxiety, by which he meant the fright or panic which occurs when an individual is actually being overwhelmed by a situation which is, or is imagined to be, catastrophic, and the other signal-anxiety, which is the response to the expectation of an impending danger. Although there are, as I shall discuss in the next chapter, difficulties attached to the idea of regarding Freud's primary anxiety as a form of anxiety, the notion of signal-anxiety is itself a perfectly straightforward one. In order to avoid primary anxiety or fright, the individual develops the capacity to perceive minimal clues of impending danger so that he can take defensive action well in advance of any actual confrontation with it. As Freud was concerned with psychopathology, the impending dangers he had in mind were psychological ones such as being overwhelmed by impulses, emotions and recollections which had previously been repressed, or being separated from objects or parts of the self without which survival is conceived to be impossible (in Freudian terminology, Separation-Anxiety and Castration Anxiety). The idea that signal-anxiety can arise in response to the threatened emergence into consciousness of parts of the individual's own mental equipment implies, of course, an antagonism between the self and its own passions, and it does indeed seem to be true that signal-anxiety is most finely developed in persons who are profoundly alienated from their instinctual and emotional nature but who have developed strong and stable personalities. In such persons the relationship between the conscious self and instinct can be neatly expressed in a metaphor which I have known patients use in dreams. A coastal town receives news that a tidal wave is approaching. The mayor orders alarm bells to be sounded and the inhabitants take all necessary precautions. The dreamer then wakes up. As a result of the evocation of signal-anxiety, which is symbolized by the sounding of alarm bells, the impending danger is dealt with before the tidal wave of instinct or emotion has come near enough for panic to ensue – or for either the patient or his analyst to discover precisely what emotion the tidal wave symbolizes. Such persons display a permanent inner-directed alertness or watchfulness which is, as it were, the mirror-image of McDougall's outward-directed Anxiety.

ANXIETY AND VIGILANCE

McDougall's Watchfulness and Freud's Signal-Anxiety are purely psychological concepts but they have an obvious connection with the biological and neurological concept of vigilance. In order to survive an organism has to be alert or awake to the possibility of changes in its environment so that it can avoid dangers and seize opportunities. Its sense-organs and nervous system have to perform the function of an ever-vigilant sentinel. This function was described by Pavlov in the following passage:

As another example of a reflex which is very much neglected we may refer to what may be called the investigatory reflex. I call it the 'What is it?' reflex. It is this reflex which brings about the immediate response in man and animals to the slightest changes in the world around them so that they immediately orient their appropriate receptor organ in accordance with the perceptible quality in the agent bringing about the change, making a full investigation of it. The biological significance of this reflex is obvious. If the animal were not provided with such a reflex its life would hang at every moment by a thread. In man this reflex has been greatly developed with far-reaching results, being represented in its highest form by inquisitiveness, the parent of the scientific method . . .

Although this is not a description of anxiety, its relation to anxiety is shown by Pavlov's statement that if it were not for the investigatory reflex 'life would hang at every moment by a thread', which is precisely what every anxious person imagines that life is just about to do. Pavlov has in fact described what might be called the resting phase of vigilance, a mere alertness to the possibility of change in the environment. If, however, a change is perceived and this change reveals the presence of something strange and unfamiliar, a more acute state of vigilance develops which can, I think, be called anxiety. Liddell, from whose paper 'The Role of Vigilance in the Development of Animal Neurosis' I have taken the preceding quotation from Pavlov, also quotes Whitehorn's description of the 'acute emotional experience':

A biological condition, characterized subjectively as an excited, tense feeling with considerable tendency to act, but with some uncertainty as to what to do, and characterized objectively by motor restlessness or activity, not smoothly patterned, with indications of excess effort, as shown in the facial and respiratory musculature, tremor of voice and of skeleto-muscular action, together with sudden changes in visceral activity. ... This experience is found, in general, to be unpleasant.

There is more than a quantitative difference between this type of vigilance and the 'What-is-it?' reflex described by Pavlov, since Whitehorn is describing the state of mind and body which develops *after* a possible danger has been perceived but *before* its nature has been understood and, therefore, before any course of action can be begun. The individual is therefore poised for action but unable to act, and is experiencing emotion without any opportunity of expressing it. As anyone who has taken an examination will know, this is how one feels after one has arrived in the examination hall but before one has read the questions – and how one feels after the results have been published but before one has found one's name on the list. This is, I think, the essence of anxiety; a danger, a problem, a test situation or an opportunity has been encountered, but its precise nature is as yet unknown and no effective action can yet be taken. The anxiety disappears the moment the situation is fully understood; one ceases to be a sentinel and becomes an agent, and the preparedness for action is replaced by action itself. This is true whatever the nature of the action, whether one goes ahead and enjoys the opportunity that has unexpectedly opened up, or copes with the problem, or ignominiously takes flight. In each case anxiety has ceased and action and some other emotion have taken its place.

SEPARATION-ANXIETY

Another statement of Liddell's is that 'vigilance minus social communication equals anxiety'. Although this statement is on the face of it untrue, since it is obviously possible to be vigilant and alone without being anxious and to be anxious while in communication with others, particularly if they are anxious too, it nonetheless draws attention to two important facts about anxiety: that it tends to be reduced by the presence of others, provided that they are both familiar and trusted, and that simultaneous exposure in infancy to stress and isolation tends to affect permanently the capacity to have normal vigilant responses. The latter appears to play an important part in the predisposition to neurotic anxiety in later life.

Liddell showed that, in the absence of their mothers, lambs of a few weeks reacted to stress by trembling and becoming passive and lethargic, in striking contrast to their twins who had been left with their mothers. These reacted to stress actively and energetically. He also showed that the separated lambs continued in later life to react feebly and 'neurotically' to stress, unlike their twins who responded energetically and purposefully.

Observations of this kind, made on both animals and human infants, have given rise to the idea that all anxiety – or at least all neurotic anxiety – is in the last resort separation-anxiety, a response to separation from a protecting, parental object rather than a reaction to unidentified danger. There are, however, objections to this idea. In the first place it is surely illogical to regard the absence of a known, protective figure rather than the presence of an unknown, threatening situation as the cause of anxiety. To do so is like attributing headaches to the absence of aspirin, or frostbite to inadequate clothing and not to exposure to extreme cold. Secondly, the young of both animals and man do not invariably become anxious if left alone; they may remain quiet and contented unless some other disturbing element is present. Thirdly, the exposure of infants and young animals to simultaneous stress and isolation is an unnatural artefact. The fact that isolated infants react to stress ineffectively is really an indication that the vigilance-responses of the immature are designed to function in concert with those of their parents; their trembling and cries of distress are presumably 'sign-stimuli' designed to evoke and potentiate vigilant responses in their mothers.

These experiments do, however, suggest that stress experienced in isolation at an age when it is natural to be protected by the mother may interfere with the normal maturation of the capacity for vigilance. As a result we have, in principle, to distinguish between two different types of neurotic anxiety: one in which the normal mechanisms of vigilance are activated by abnormal stimuli, as in the case of signal-anxiety evoked by the threatened emergence of repressed impulses and phobic anxiety evoked by inappropriate external stimuli, and another in which the mechanisms of vigilance misfire – leading to trembling, dithering and 'going to pieces' instead of to heightened alertness and greater efficiency.*

It should also be mentioned here that – for reasons which will emerge in Chapter 5 – neurotics who are phobic and hysterical do not believe that they are entitled to assume responsibility for their own lives. They therefore behave as though they still need parental protection and when anxious react in a way which is unconsciously designed to evoke protective responses in others rather than to save the situation themselves. In other words, neurotic dependence manifests itself in an inability to rely on the self's own capacity for

* According to the Yerkes–Dodson Law, anxiety increases efficiency until it reaches a certain threshold of intensity, after which it reduces it, but it is possible that this threshold is a function not only of the intensity of the anxiety but also of the integrity of vigilance-mechanisms, and that infantile traumata of the kind to be discussed in the next chapter may lower the threshold at which anxiety ceases to enhance efficiency.

vigilance and a resulting need to evoke vigilance and anxiety in others.

Anxiety, then, is the expectation of something as yet unknown. Since the unknown for human beings includes alienated unconscious parts of themselves, this as-yet-unknown may be either inside or outside themselves and the same emotion, anxiety, may be evoked by either subjective or objective occurrences. Since knowledge is incompatible with anxiety, though not, of course, with despondency or despair, the drive to know, 'inquisitiveness, the parent of the scientific method', may be regarded as a way of trying to eliminate anxiety. As Liddell puts it, 'anxiety accompanies intellectual activity as its shadow', an aphorism which derives much of its point from the fact that knowledge has an awkward habit of revealing unexpected areas of ignorance and therefore tends to engender the anxiety which it sets out to reduce.

The fact that anxiety is evoked by the as-yet-unknown means that all novel experiences tend to be preceded by anxiety. The first day at school or in a new job, the first night or holiday spent away from one's family, the first sexual intercourse, giving birth to one's first child, one's first contact with serious illness or death, are all encounters with novel circumstances, sensations and emotions for which one's previous life cannot fully have prepared one; they therefore tend to evoke anxiety, regardless of whether one anticipates that the experience will be pleasurable or distressing.

Chapter 2

Anxiety, Fright
and Shock

In the previous chapter I have argued that anxiety is that
form of vigilance which occurs after one has encountered a
danger, problem or opportunity but before one has become
aware of its precise nature and thus before one knows whether
one is still on familiar territory. As Sir Charles Sherrington
has put it: 'A shell of its immediate future surrounds the
animal's head. The nerve-nets in the head are therefore busy
with signals from a shell of the outside world which the
animal is about to enter and experience.' I am suggesting that
anxiety occurs when this shell of the immediate future is
found to contain something which is unrecognized and
which cannot therefore be evaluated immediately.

I have also argued that certain forms of anxiety, notably
neurotic apprehensiveness and over-anxious concern, are the
result of inward-looking vigilance or signal-anxiety encoun-
tering signs of the stirring of repressed, and therefore
unconscious, mental activity: stirrings which the individual
treats as coming from outside himself and to which he
reacts as though they were potentially dangerous.

This definition of anxiety as a form of expectancy makes it
possible to distinguish between anxiety and a number of

other emotions with which it tends to be confused, particularly perhaps by psychiatrists and psycho-analysts. I refer to such emotions as Fright, Panic, Shock and Trauma, all of which can be regarded as the effects of a failure of anxiety to fulfil its function of alerting the individual. In this chapter I shall argue that Fright and Panic occur when anxiety has been aroused too late for the individual to avoid direct confrontation with some danger, and that Shock and Trauma occur when something totally unexpected happens so that 'the shell of one's immediate future' is invaded without any premonitory signs which could have evoked vigilance and anxiety.

I have already mentioned that Freud drew a distinction between signal-anxiety and primary anxiety, which he also called automatic anxiety, and that he regarded signal-anxiety as a device for avoiding primary anxiety; this primary anxiety being the distressing emotion which occurs when one is actually being overwhelmed by the dangerous experience which the capacity for signal-anxiety has been developed to avoid. In making this distinction in the way he did Freud was, to my mind, using the word anxiety to embrace three different experiences – apprehensiveness, fright and shock – in a way that is not possible, at least in English. If one searches *Roget's Thesaurus* for synonyms for anxiety one finds only one reference to its use to describe an emotion relating to a present experience. This is where it is classified among the 'Personal Passive Affections – Pain' and is listed as a synonym for care and solicitude. The other references are all to the future, the three other categories in which the word anxiety is listed being 'Extension of Thought to the Future – Expectation', 'Personal Prospective Affections – Desire' and 'Personal Prospective Affections – Fear'. The one reference in which the emphasis is on the present, however, gives no sanction for its use to describe the sort of phenomenon Freud had in mind when he formulated the concept of primary anxiety. The pain of care and solicitude is the distress of one person over the suffering of another, while the pain of automatic anxiety is that of the self experiencing its own disintegration.

The tendency of Freud and other psycho-analysts to regard fright and panic as forms of anxiety derives in part from the fact that Freud wrote in German. '*Angst*', the German word used by Freud, is regularly translated into English as 'anxiety', but it has, it seems, a meaning which is in some ways closer to that of the English word 'anguish' and evokes the ideas of distress and fear more readily than it does that of expectancy. The English translation of Freud indeed frequently uses the phrase 'expectant anxiety' which, to my mind, is a tautology. The intransitive use of the word 'anxious' to refer to people who are what an older generation used to call 'nervy' or 'highly-strung' appears, incidentally, to be of fairly recent origin, and presumably reflects the contemporary tendency to prefer psychological to physiological explanations of temperament.

There is, however, another and more substantial reason for the tendency to regard anxiety and fright as experiences of the same order. This is the fact that in any situation short of death there is always something worse that can happen. As a result, not only is apprehensive anxiety the expectation that something frightening may happen, but the apprehension that even worse may befall one is also part of Fright. Fright and Panic are therefore forms of anxiety to the extent that they include expectation of the as-yet-unknown in the form of dread of annihilation.

ANXIETY AND FRIGHT

If the biological function of anxiety is to enable the individual to anticipate danger, the emotion of fright will only occur if anxiety has been aroused too late for the individual to take appropriate avoiding action. Although there is a tendency when talking loosely to regard anxiety, fright and terror as merely increasing intensities of fear, consideration of a particular instance shows that there are in fact qualitative differences between these three emotions. If one imagines oneself first on a country walk, then seeing an animal in the same field as oneself which might be a bull, then noticing that it is in fact a bull, then being charged by it, and finally being gored by it, one will be able to imagine oneself going through a series of three or possibly four distinct emotions. First one will be calm and oblivious of the fact that one is maintaining the state of vigilance which enables one to notice that one has entered a field in which there is an animal which might be a bull. Then one notices that it is a bull and becomes anxious, being uncertain as to whether one has been noticed by the bull and not knowing whether it will charge or whether one still has time to beat a hasty retreat. Then it charges; one knows quite well what the danger is and becomes frightened. Finally it overtakes one and one becomes terrified. Furthermore, at some point another qualitative change will occur. The anxiety or fear will cease to be manageable and will no longer act as a spur to intelligent avoiding action but will be replaced by panic, in the sense of precipitate flight, or perhaps by paralysis. The point at which vigilance will turn into anxiety, anxiety into fear, and fear into panic or terror, will, of course, depend upon the age, temperament and previous experience of the person exposed to danger. A town-bred child might remain oblivious of the danger until the bull had actually begun to charge him and go rapidly from generalized vigilance to terror. A neurotic might assume that all cattle were bulls and become anxious the moment he noticed the animal, while a farmer might believe in his capacity to handle the situation and only become anxious at a very late stage in the disaster, but at some point in this hypothetical situation everyone would cease to experience anxiety and would instead find himself in a terrifying present.

The fact that this transition from vigilance and anxiety to

terror and panic is dependent on knowledge, experience and temperament is, of course, generally recognized and is taken into account in the selection and training of personnel for dangerous occupations. One's preference for being in a car driven by an experienced driver is based on one's expectation that his vigilance will only rarely change into anxiety and that his anxiety will even more rarely turn into panic. It is, however, perhaps less generally realized that panic occurs sooner and more frequently in foolhardy persons who refuse to admit that they are ever anxious and who are therefore less vigilant and more prone to be taken by surprise, not only by unexpected hazards but also by their own emotional reactions to them. In both the last two wars it was noticed that soldiers who boasted that they would never be scared in action were more likely to break down than those who appreciated that warfare is frightening and were well aware of their own susceptibility to fear.

ANXIETY AND SHOCK

In the hypothetical example cited above I envisaged a situation of mounting danger and anxiety in which the danger is perceived before it is imminent. I suggested that the culmination of anxiety and fear is terror and panic, by which I mean the suspension of intelligent action and its replacement by the purely reflex response of flight. In such cases anxiety and vigilance have failed in their function of enabling the individual to avoid direct confrontation with danger. There is, however, another class of experience in which vigilance fails, not by being aroused too late but by not being aroused at all, in which something totally unexpected happens without any warning signs having entered the shell of one's immediate future.

This type of failure of vigilance leads to the experience of shock. In the psychiatric literature shock is always discussed in terms of the unexpected unpleasant experience, such an occurrence being termed a trauma; but before considering traumatic experiences it is perhaps worth mentioning the fact that unexpected events can also be pleasant or neutral and that they have a curiously disconcerting or shocking quality which is momentarily unpleasant. The typical immediate reaction to totally unexpected good news is first incredulity and then a bustle of activity in which one anxiously confirms that the recipient of the unexpected legacy is really oneself, or that the unexpected visitor is really the son one imagined to be abroad. One needs time to get used to the good news and experiences retrospectively some of the agitation and restlessness that one would have experienced in anticipation if one had been forewarned. One has not been prepared for the event either by anxiety or vigilance and one needs time to re-orientate oneself and get used to the idea of living in a different future to the one that had been expected.

Another example of the totally unexpected experience is that of being given a turn or a start by suddenly finding someone standing beside us when we have believed ourselves to be alone. This is disconcerting even if the person taking us by surprise is someone familiar, and we usually react to it by momentarily becoming tense, saying 'You did give me a start' and then relaxing again. Although this is an experience which we have all had, I have the impression that it occurs more readily to people when they are in a daydream or brown study than it does to people who are concentrating on some actual task. In the former state one has ceased to be vigilant in relation to the external world, which has temporarily ceased to be real. Joseph Breuer, Freud's original collaborator, held that 'hypnoid states', in which the individual is no longer in full waking contact with the outside world, were an essential prerequisite for the traumatic experiences which he and Freud originally maintained were the cause of hysteria. According to Breuer these hypnoid states occurred typically in women who spent much of their time engaged in household tasks which did not engage their full attention and who were therefore liable to get lost in day-dreams.

Although these examples of being startled by unexpected pleasant or neutral occurrences are of some interest in showing to what extent our capacity to function smoothly and retain our serenity is dependent on there being some correspondence between what we anticipate may happen and what actually does, the totally unexpected, unpleasant experience is of much greater practical importance, since it can lead to reactions which may for a while be incapacitating. This type of occurrence is known technically as a traumatic experience, the concept of trauma being borrowed from general medicine where it signifies an injury to the body resulting from external violence. A broken bone, a cut finger and concussion are all physical traumata, the features common to them being that their cause is a collision between the body and an external object, that the result is some disruption of the integrity of the body, and that recovery occurs by a spontaneous process of healing at a tempo set by the body's health and capacity for regrowth. Psychiatrists have borrowed the concept of trauma to describe analogous psychological occurrences, viz. those which happen unexpectedly and without the individual's own will being in any way implicated, which disrupt the individual's integrity and sense of continuity of being, and from which recovery occurs by a process of gradually assimilating the experience, the rate of recovery being dependent on the individual's age, maturity, stability and freedom from other preoccupations.

The immediate response to a traumatic experience is a mixture of confusion, shock and fright, the confusion and shock being due to the traumatic event's unexpectedness and intensity, and the fright to the fact that, by definition, the traumatic experience, insofar as its nature is apprehended at all, must be frightening. Fright is, however, often entirely absent and most observers of disasters have been impressed by the lack of any emotion whatsoever in the survivors.

Alexander N. Hood, who recorded his 'Personal Experiences in the Great Earthquake' at Messina in 1909, observed that

The immediate and almost universal effect that the earthquake had on those who escaped death at Messina was of stupefaction, almost of mental paralysis. . . . Lamentation was infrequently heard except when caused by physical suffering. Tears were rarely seen. Men recounted how they had lost wife, mother, brothers, sisters, children and all their possessions, with no apparent concern. They told their tales of woe as if they themselves had been disinterested spectators of another's loss.*

Some but not all of those who survive totally unexpected disasters such as earthquakes and train accidents develop the condition known to psychiatrists as traumatic neurosis. In those who do, the initial state of shock and stupefaction is followed by symptoms of three different kinds: general incapacity, in the sense that the victim cannot work or concentrate and loses sexual desire; emotional spells, in which he is restless and agitated, is liable to cry, shout and lose his temper about trivialities; and waking actions and dreams in which the traumatic experience is repeated.

This repetition of the experience consists partly of going over the event again and again in the mind and partly of performing gestures which correspond to actions which the person either did or might usefully have performed during it. Kardiner cites the case of a man who, some years after the First World War, had a tic which on investigation proved to be part of the movement of putting on a gas-mask. In fact the man had not been able to put on his gas-mask before the gas attack which proved to be a traumatic experience for him. In addition persons suffering from a traumatic neurosis have recurrent nightmares in which they re-experience the traumatic event.

Although these later effects of the trauma are on the face of it the symptoms of the traumatic neurosis, they are better thought of as manifestations of the healing process. By

* Quoted by Martha Wolfenstein in *Disaster*.

repeating the trauma the traumatized person is, as it were, trying to get it in front of himself again so that he can anticipate it, react anxiously to it and then assimilate or 'get over' it in the way that he would any other distressing experience. During the period of imaginative retrospective confrontation he experiences the anxiety that would have preceded the traumatic experience if he had known it was coming.

Traumatic neuroses resemble physical traumata in that they tend to recover with time and rest, provided the patient is psychologically healthy and wishes to recover. The latter is an important proviso, since in wartime recovery may mean return to active service and in peacetime it may mean sacrificing the chance of a disability pension. As a result, a certain number of traumatic neuroses turn into compensation neuroses, in which the patient sacrifices his mental health – and his self-respect – for the sake of physical safety or material security, and it is usually impossible to decide to what extent the patient is aware of his motive for remaining ill. In civil cases recovery is more likely if the victim of a trauma is awarded damages than if he is granted a pension which is contingent on his remaining ill. The following item taken from *The Evening Standard* (10 March 1965) describes vividly a typical traumatic experience and the kinds of symptoms to which it may give rise.

Nightmares after rail crash – £300 for wife · Evening Standard Reporter

A young housewife who was injured in a railway accident in December 1963 started to have frequent nightmares and became afraid to travel on a train, the High Court was told today.

Mrs Jean Margaret Bradfield sued British Railways. She was awarded £300 damages.

The Board admitted liability and only contested the issue of damages claimed by Mrs Bradfield.

Mr R. Gavin Freeman, for Mrs Bradfield, said the axle broke on the crowded Chadwell Heath–Liverpool Street train.

The carriage overturned. Mrs Bradfield was sitting on the offside and was at the bottom of a pile of screaming and crying people. She remained like that for twenty minutes in complete darkness.

Now she had nightmares not every night but fairly frequently. Her attitude was: 'I know it's silly to be frightened to go in a train, but I am frightened. I know I will get over it, but at the present moment I am terrified.'

Mrs Bradfield told Mr Justice Paull that there were quite a few people standing in the train. 'One moment I was sitting . . . then I found myself lying on the floor with a lot of "bodies" on top of me. I still have nightmares. It's silly but I do.'

She said that she now changed trains at Stratford and caught an Underground train because of her aversion to go into Liverpool Street Station.

The judge said: 'I quite understand. You don't like going over the stretch of line on which the accident happened.'

Surprisingly little seems to be known about the factors which determine whether a person is likely to develop a traumatic neurosis if confronted by a totally unexpected disaster, except that highly-strung and anxious people do not seem to be more susceptible than the stolid and phlegmatic. Kardiner's study of traumatic neurosis suggests, however, that neurotics with highly-controlled and rigid personalities may be more susceptible than those who are habitually anxious. Presumably those who are accustomed to feeling insecure are less liable to be traumatized than those whose personality is set to the assumption that they are always in a position to control themselves and their environment, in the same way that buildings with a certain amount of give in them withstand tornadoes and earthquakes better than those that are rigidly constructed.

Traumatic neuroses and traumatic dreams are of considerable theoretical interest in that they are not susceptible to psycho-analytical and symbolic interpretation, since the symptoms and dream-images of traumatic neurosis are undisguised reproductions of the actual causative event. As a result traumatic neurosis is the one form of psychological illness for which interpretative psychotherapy is not indicated, and Freud, in his last book, *An Outline of Psycho-Analysis*

(1940), remarked with evident regret that 'their relations to childhood determinants have hitherto eluded investigation'. However, psychotherapists not infrequently encounter patients who appear to have had traumatic experiences in their childhood or adolescence and the tendency of traumatic experiences to be repeated in such patients is shown by a curious change in the patient's behaviour. Instead of remembering and recounting the past, he re-enacts it. He replaces the past tense by the present and adopts the postures and uses the gestures which he used at the time of the original traumatic event, even though he may have no conscious recollection of, say, the surgical operation for which his parents and doctor thought it best not to prepare him.

Traumatic neurosis also differs from other forms of neurosis in that it is explicable in terms of a single and easily ascertained event occurring in adult life, whereas the other neuroses appear to originate in childhood and can only exceptionally be attributed to one single traumatic experience. The response of children to totally unexpected distressing events differs from that of adults in at least two respects; firstly, it occurs during the period in which personality is developing and is likely to become part and parcel of a distortion of the whole personality instead of remaining a foreign body external to it, and secondly, the helplessness and emotional dependence of children means that they are likely to be traumatized by unexpected events in the realm of their personal attachments, such as the death or sudden departure of their parents, rather than by impersonal disasters such as earthquakes and railway accidents. As a result, trauma in childhood – infantile trauma as it is called technically – differs radically from trauma in adult life and raises problems about the origins of neurosis which entitle it to a section to itself.

INFANTILE TRAUMA AND THE ORIGINS OF NEUROSIS

The idea that neurosis is the result of infantile traumatic experiences implies that children are highly susceptible to being traumatized. This gives rise to no particular difficulties since their helplessness, inexperience and immaturity makes it likely that things will happen to them which they can neither anticipate, avoid nor understand. It also implies that there are a number of common, perhaps even universal, childhood experiences which can be adduced as likely traumatic agents. This latter assumption is necessary since neurosis is too common to be explicable as the result of experiences of a kind only rarely encountered by children. The traumatic theory of neurosis implies, therefore, that it is not uncommon, perhaps even usual, for children to grow up in an environment which overtaxes their capacity to understand and accept painful and frustrating events, and in which they not infrequently encounter experiences before they are mature enough to assimilate them. Since unimaginative parents are not exactly a rarity, this is not, in itself, an improbable assumption, though it does, of course, raise the question of how some children go through seemingly disastrous experiences without becoming neurotic, which is ultimately the same problem as that of explaining why some adults go through disasters without developing a traumatic neurosis.

The great attraction of the traumatic theory of neurosis for Freud and for the majority of psycho-analysts since him is that it enables psycho-analytical theory to be fitted into the scientific frame of reference without any of the modifications which its peculiar subject-matter might seem to necessitate. Freud believed in what he called the principle of psychic determinism, according to which mental events have causes in exactly the same sense that physical events do, and the traumatic theory of neurosis enabled him to apply the concept of causation directly to neurotic phenomena;

the traumatic experience could be adduced as the cause of the neurosis and the symptoms could be regarded as its inevitable effect. However, this way of looking at neurosis encounters considerable difficulties if it is worked out in detail.

In the first place it eliminates the notion of choice, since it assumes that neurosis is the result of something that happened to the patient when he was a child and that he was in no way a participator or creator of the circumstances that traumatized him. That this was an objection to the theory did not emerge so long as psycho-analysis confined its attention to the elucidation of symptoms but began to become apparent when it became imperialistic and expanded its territory to include not only the causation of neuroses but also the development of the whole personality. It then laid itself open to the charge that as well as explaining psychologically aspects of personality that might well be hereditary or constitutional, it was assuming that people, and not just their neuroses, are simply the result of what has happened to them, that all acts of choice and decision are an illusion and that human beings in no way create the world they live in. This elimination of the idea that human beings can be agents actively choosing, deciding and creating is not only, arguably, immoral, since it encourages the idea that one is responsible for none of one's acts, but also logically untenable, since it implies that consciousness is an epiphenomenon without function; and yet psycho-analytical therapy is based on the assumption that making unconscious mental processes conscious enables the individual to free himself of the compulsion to repeat childhood patterns of behaviour. Scepticism as to the validity of explaining individual behaviour solely in terms of past passively received experience has led in the U.S.A. – and to a lesser extent in this country – to the development of theories of psychological interaction, in which it is assumed that all members of a group such as the family, even the children, actively influence one another, and that the disturbed or neurotic behaviour of any one member can only be understood in terms of the dynamics of the whole group.

In the second place, the traumatic theory of neurosis raises the problem of deciding which are in fact the traumatic experiences of childhood, and this has proved so difficult that it would be possible to write the history of psycho-analysis in terms of various kinds of shocking or frightening experience which have been cast for the role of prime traumatic agent. The list of nominees for this position includes sexual seduction by adults, which Freud abandoned when he realized that his patients had been telling him fantasies and not recollections; the so-called birth-trauma, originally propounded by Otto Rank and accepted for a while with reservations by Freud, which tried to explain the human propensity to anxiety by referring it to a universally experienced shocking event; the discovery of the anatomical differences between the sexes which, it was inferred, led to fear of castration in boys and in girls to the conviction that they had already been castrated; separation from the mother in infancy leading to anxiety derived from the infant's recognition of its own helplessness and separateness; and fear of being overwhelmed by the strength of one's own impulses, this last being of a different order to the others since it refers not to the impact of the outside world on the child but to its sensing a disparity of strength between different parts of itself. Although the sexual seduction and birth trauma varieties of the traumatic theory of neurosis have died a natural death, the other three have proved viable concepts. But I doubt whether many contemporary analysts would maintain that any one of the other three was either *the* cause of neurosis in general or was the sole cause of any particular neurosis. The possible exception is the idea that separation from the mother in infancy is the cause of neurosis, but even Bowlby, Fairbairn and Winnicott, the three English analysts who have most emphasized the importance of separation-anxiety and maternal deprivation as a cause of neurosis, would not maintain that neurosis was the result of a single, unexpected separation from the mother. Although Winnicott in particular often uses the word trauma, all three have been more concerned to elucidate what really goes on between an infant and its mother and in what ways failures and inadequacies of mothering may affect the infant's later emotional development than to demonstrate that separation from the mother is a traumatic experience in the strict sense of the term.

Naive traumatic theories of neurosis fail therefore because they ignore the part played by children in influencing their environment and in selecting their own experiences – the so-called 'victims' of sexual assaults are not uncommonly willing participants or even themselves the seducers (see Mohr, Turner and Jerry's *Pedophilia and Exhibitionism*) – and because they tend to be pancrestons (universal explanatory hypotheses) which fail to explain anything in particular because they can be used to explain everything, but these objections do not apply to the more sophisticated idea that non-correspondence between the rate of mental development of a child and the rate of change and complication of its environment may contribute towards the susceptibility to neurosis. This idea, which lies at the back of much of Bowlby's and Winnicott's writings, preserves the notion of infantile trauma by extending it to include not only experiences which shatter the integrity of the child and produce a traumatic neurosis proper but also those which compel it to use protective measures (defences) to preserve its integrity. The first step in self-defence is the development of signal-anxiety, which on the principle of 'once bitten, twice shy', enables the child to avoid both re-exposure to the traumatic situation and recollection of the original one – or, if the situation is one which cannot be avoided, to develop a protective shell or carapace which enables it to act as though it were oblivious of whatever it is in its environment that it finds hurtful. Winnicott calls this shell 'the false self' and he regards it as a front of superficial conformity and happiness behind which the child preserves his potential spontaneity and sensibility.

This extended traumatic theory of neurosis makes shock, not anxiety or fear, the prime mover in neurosis since it assumes that the essential quality of experiences which evoke defences is that they are unexpected and incomprehensible. Although Winnicott does not use the concept shock he frequently uses the phrase 'environmental impingement' to refer to experiences which the child or infant cannot comprehend and which lead to what Winnicott calls 'snapping of the thread of continuity of the self'.

This is most obviously true in the case of birth. It is a purely speculative notion that infants are anxious or afraid while they are being born, but it is a physiological certainty that it is totally unlike anything that they have experienced before and that it demands a massive re-orientation of their whole mode of being and that all infants experience a greater or lesser degree of physiological shock. Similarly, it is by no means obvious why discovery of the anatomical differences between the sexes should in itself arouse fear or anxiety, but it is certainly a discovery which adds a new dimension to the child's conception of the world and which, to put it mildly, taxes both its intelligence and its imagination. That the problem of sexual enlightenment is essentially one of ensuring that a child is not confronted with more than its capacity for anxiety and vigilance will enable it to master is taken into account in the advice usually given to parents that their children's questions should be answered simply and that the answers should not go into greater detail than the actual questions demand. In this way a child can itself determine the extent and timing of its discovery of the facts of life and can avoid the shock or pathological impingement of being forced to get puzzled and upset about something that it is not yet ready to understand.

Lasting separation from parents or their loss by death is, I suspect, only traumatic if either the child is so young that the idea of 'going away' cannot yet be connected with that of 'coming back' (or in the case of loss by death, if the child is too young for there to be any possibility of it retaining a living memory of the dead parent) or the child is neither forewarned that the event may occur nor given any opportunity to express its feelings afterwards. Many grown-ups seem to have no idea that children can experience grief or that a bereavement is 'got over' better and sooner if grief is expressed openly and shared with others. The apparent unconcern which is displayed by some children who remain unvisited in hospital or who have recently been bereaved, and which so often deceives unimaginative adults into thinking that the child 'is taking it very well', should really be regarded as a manifestation of its 'false self' and as an indication that it has developed defences to prevent it being overwhelmed by greater grief than it can endure – or than it believes those around it could tolerate.

The point I am making here is that the so-called infantile trauma probably owes its harmful effects not simply to the fact that it is distressing but to the fact that it is unexpected and unimaginable, and that it has therefore not been preceded by anxiety and vigilance. An infantile traumatic experience is one which was not represented in the shell of the child's immediate future nor in his general scheme of the nature of reality. It is something which makes the bottom fall out of his world and which compels him either to recognize precociously the uncertainty and insecurity of the human condition, in which case he will grow up wise and unhappy but not ill, or to institute defences to enable him to deny that the disillusioning disaster has really occurred, in which case he will unconsciously shy away from anything that might remind him of the trauma, and become, as I shall explain in a later chapter, an inhibited person and a potential neurotic.

NIGHTMARES

Another example of a shocking and frightening experience which is not preceded by anxiety is the nightmare. Although all dreams are totally unexpected events in the sense that no one has ever succeeded in predicting what he or anyone else will dream – though recent experimental research has made it possible to predict when someone will dream – nightmares differ from other dreams in that the mechanism of signal-anxiety for some unknown reason fails to operate. In most dreams, even those which are unpleasant, the dreamer retains sufficient vigilance to prevent the dream from getting out of hand, either by saying to himself 'but it's only a dream' or by waking himself before anything frightening actually happens. This continued action, even in sleep, of inward-directed vigilance, is presumably due to the fact that most dreams occur in the so-called 'paradoxical phase of sleep' which combines some of the features of deep sleep with those of awakening, but I know of no evidence suggesting that nightmares occur only in non-paradoxical phases of sleep. The action of signal-anxiety in preventing a dream turning into a nightmare is well illustrated by the dream I quoted in Chapter 1 in which signal-anxiety was itself represented and in which the dreamer woke up before he was anywhere near imagining himself face-to-face with the tidal wave, and I think that most people have had dreams from which they have awoken before confronting some danger or performing some frightening task that the dream setting seemed to demand of them.

Another way in which the full impact of a frightening dream may be mitigated is by failing to remember it until after its objective untruth has been demonstrated. The Italian poet Leopardi has recorded in his poem 'The Terror by Night' a dream which he had of the moon falling out of the sky and crashing to the ground, which he only remembered after he had noticed that the moon was still in its proper place. In this instance a true nightmare has been avoided by the defensive manoeuvre of forgetting the dream until it is broken by a waking perception which invalidates its frightening content and proves that the disaster depicted in the dream cannot really have taken place. I have published a detailed analysis of this dream elsewhere.

In the true nightmare, however, signal-anxiety, for whatever reason, fails to operate and the dreamer is awakened not by anxiety but by fright and it usually takes him some time to realize that, objectively speaking, nothing has happened. Nightmares occur fairly commonly in children, partly because they have greater difficulty than adults in distinguishing between imaginative activity and true perception and have not yet subscribed to the adult convention that dreams are mere trivialities, and partly because they have less control over their own impulses and are therefore in greater danger of being overwhelmed by feelings which they are trying, as yet unsuccessfully, to repress and disown. The fear of being overwhelmed by the strength of one's own impulses, to which I referred in the previous section, is the price paid by children for identifying with the process of domestication which will enable them to become civilized adults. It is, I suspect, the future neurotics and not the future delinquents who suffer from nightmares.

Nightmares also occur in adults but only, I think, if they are in a state of acute conflict about matters of which they are totally unconscious. A young man, who had never had any reason to regard himself as neurotic, consulted a psychotherapist on account of a recurrent nightmare from which he awoke drenched in sweat several nights a week. He had never been a prolific dreamer and the subject-matter of the dream, let alone its meaning, was totally incomprehensible to him. He was falling into some complex machinery, was already caught up in it and only awoke at the moment at which he was about to be dismembered. By a lucky chance the psychotherapist was able to identify the machinery immediately; it was a composite of a threshing machine and the type of electricity generating plant that used to be common on country estates before the advent of the National Grid. When this was pointed out to the young man, he recognized it immediately and said that he had spent his childhood on his father's estate, where both objects had been familiar to him. The nightmare had now ceased to be totally mysterious, its imagery had become located in familiar territory, and the nightmares ceased before his psychotherapist had ventured on any interpretation of the meaning of a dream of becoming entangled and almost destroyed by one's father's threshing machine and generating plant. It was only in later sessions that it became apparent that his nightmares had started after he had accepted without protest his father's plans for his future, even though these bore no relation to his own inclinations and aptitudes. Coming of a tradition which accepts paternal authority as natural, he had had no idea that he had been in any way disturbed by renouncing his own wishes in favour of his father's. The nightmare was, one might say, due to a failure of vigilance and self-awareness in respect of the inevitable and age-old conflict between fathers and sons. As a result he was taken totally unawares by the threat to his integrity to which his compliance, loyalty and filial respect had exposed him.

Chapter 3

Anxiety, Guilt
and Depression

In the two previous chapters I have discussed the general
nature of anxiety and its relation to fright and shock, two
emotions which clearly resemble it in having physical
manifestations and in being as readily observable in animals
as in man. In this chapter I shall discuss its relation to two
other emotions, guilt and depression, which are psychologically more complex and which are probably specifically
human emotions. Although one might assert that a dog
looked guilty or depressed, I do not think that anyone would
maintain that an animal is guilty or depressed with the same
assurance that he would that one is frightened or shocked –
or that he himself felt guilty and depressed.

In this chapter, then, we shall be concerned exclusively
with human psychology and psychopathology and with
states of mind that we know of only by introspection and
empathy. As a result I shall not be able to quote physiological descriptions of guilt and depression in the way that I was
able to quote Pavlov and Whitehorn on vigilance. This is
unfortunate, since severe depression is undoubtedly accompanied by physiological changes, but there appears to be no
normal counterpart to depression occurring in animals.

Attempts have been made to conceive of human depression as an analogue of animal hibernation, but although it includes a general depression of vital activity, hibernation is more like sleep than depression and is a quiet and presumably painless state, whereas human depression is a painful, agitated and restless state of both body and mind and is usually accompanied by insomnia. Nor can the pining of animals when isolated from their kind or kept in captivity really be regarded as similar to depression in man; it is more like actual unhappiness and despair.

My reason for considering the relation of anxiety to guilt and depression is practical and clinical. In both health and illness anxiety, guilt and depression are experienced together and those who seek psychological help so frequently complain of feeling two or three of these emotions that it is necessary to think of them as an interrelated triad. This is reflected in the way in which psychological and psychoanalytical theories tend to explain and define them in terms of one another. The close association of these three emotions is also remarkable in that anxiety would appear, at first sight, to be incompatible with both guilt and depression, since anxiety is directed towards the future while guilt refers typically to the past and, while anxiety heightens vitality, depression lowers it.

GUILT AND INTERNALIZATION

We are here concerned with guilt as a state of mind, not guilt as a legal concept. Legal guilt is a question of fact not of feeling and a person is legally guilty if he has transgressed the law quite regardless of whether he knows that he has done so or whether he feels guilty about having done so. However, owing to the fact that society has formulated the law, which therefore has the weight of authority behind it, there is a tendency for people to feel guilty when they are legally guilty. There are, however, numerous exceptions to this tendency. The offence may be too trivial – I doubt whether many people actually feel guilty about feeding a parking meter – or too technical, as in the case of some forms of tax evasion. Nor do people in general feel guilty about breaking laws of which they do not themselves approve. Indeed, under certain circumstances, notably in tyrannical and totalitarian societies, an individual may feel guilty about obeying the law and may find it necessary to break the law if he is to retain his self-respect. There are also people who are, or appear to be, immune to feeling guilty and whose social conformity is determined by fear and not by guilt.

The emotion of guilt is evoked by actions – and in some people even by thoughts – which offend against whatever authority or authorities the individual identifies himself with – or has *internalized*. Internalization is the technical term for that process by which the individual constructs a mental representation of the outside world and of the people in it and thereafter reacts to these mental representations as though they had some of the force and reality of the external figures themselves. It is the dependence of guilt on internalization which explains why it is hardly, if at all, developed among animals and why we find it impossible to imagine an infant feeling guilty. Animals and infants have little if any capacity for symbolic thought and are therefore incapable of reflecting upon the consequences of their actions, or of remaining convinced of the reality of beings who are not physically present, and still less of conceiving that the interests or demands of others are more important than the satisfaction of their own wishes. Only after a child has come to appreciate the otherness of others and can retain an image of them in their absence, does the possibility of its experiencing guilt or concern arise, these two emotions differing, I think, in that concern relates to others who are felt to be human and equal to oneself while guilt relates to figures who are felt to be of a higher order than oneself. Disobedience to parents, or God, or betrayal of an ideal, may produce guilt, while injury to an equal will evoke concern. It is, however, not always possible to differentiate guilt and concern as clearly as this formulation would suggest, since injuring an equal usually also involves an infringement of the moral ideal that one should never harm others.

The dependence of guilt on internalization and the development of symbolic thinking is responsible for the fact that guilt is experienced in its most exquisite forms by persons such as intellectuals, academics and religieux who are mentally highly developed and who appear to be able to dispense for long periods with direct human contact. Unreflective, feckless people, on the other hand, crave continuous human contact but are, in general, conspicuous for their lack of any sense of guilt. The past for them is over and done with and lacks sufficient reality to be the subject of guilt and remorse. This is one of the reasons why punishment, which is usually inflicted long after commission of a crime, so rarely has any reformative effect.

The sense of guilt, then, is dependent on internalization and indicates the existence of a conflict between two parts of the self, one of which, the egotistic part, says 'I want to' while the other, the internalized authority, says 'I ought not to'; or, alternatively, 'I did' and 'I ought not to have'. This conflict is not necessarily neurotic. In the same way as anxiety is an emotion necessary for physical survival which only becomes neurotic if it is evoked by situations which do not objectively call for increased vigilance, so guilt is an emotion necessary for social harmony which only becomes neurotic if it is evoked by situations in which there is no real clash of interests and values between oneself and society. In contemporary society, which in peacetime, at least, sets a high value on the sanctity of life, it would, I think, be neurotic not to feel guilty if one was responsible for someone else's death. It would be nice to believe that an inherent sense of guilt attached to the idea of killing another human being, but the facts really seem to be against this. People rarely seem to feel guilty about killing members of the enemy in wartime though they do usually demand that their acts of homicide be justified by some ideal and blessed by the appropriate spiritual authority. Guilt seems to arise only if the victim is experienced as a member of the group with which one feels identified, and this group is usually smaller than the human race and often smaller than the nation of which one is nominally a member, as is shown by the fact that civil wars are, if one takes the whole world into account, not infrequent events. Under certain historical circumstances, indeed, and among certain groups, pride, dynastic ambition and self-interest may be valued more highly than respect for life and people may be prepared to kill members of their own class and even family, without apparently feeling guilt. Although the Plantagenets and Tudors were usually keen to legalize their dynastic murders, they were not, so far as one knows, unduly troubled by the guilt and remorse, which would, one hopes, deter our present political leaders if they were ever tempted to behave in the same way.

Guilt about killing is, of course, an – perhaps the – extreme case but the same principle applies to deeds less final and dramatic than murder. Since the sense of guilt depends on the internalization of social values and ideals it is impossible to assess whether someone has a moral or neurotic sense of guilt unless one is familiar with the culture in which he lives and understands every nuance of its system of values. There are, indeed, great difficulties in appreciating the sense of guilt of persons with different values to oneself. It requires an imaginative leap for an entirely secular person to appreciate the sense of guilt about failures in religious observance that may afflict a practising Christian and a sense of social history to realize that many middle-aged men of the English upper and middle classes feel guilty about not being able to provide their wives with servants in the style that was usual in their own childhood.

However, as the sense of guilt is only evoked in situations

of conflict, it tends to be evoked more frequently and intensely in persons who have internalized their authorities out of fear than in those who have internalized them out of love. The person who has been brought up by parents and teachers who have enforced their will and instilled their values by fear is more likely to be plagued by a sense of guilt than those who have been brought up kindly and who have incorporated the values of authority figures whom they loved and admired. The former bears a grudge against authority and wishes unconsciously to defy it, however much he may consciously subscribe to its values. His whole attitude towards values is, indeed, corrupted by a conflict between a wish to defy authority as such and a fear-inspired need to submit to it, which stands in the way of his ever making a genuine moral judgement or stand. This conflict tends to produce a vicious circle, since his defiance will make him frightened and increase his need to submit and his submission will increase his hostility and make him defiant. In severe cases this conflict leads to the condition known to psychiatry as obsessional neurosis, in which the patient feels compelled to think or do things which are totally foreign to his conscious conforming personality; every thought and action becomes an agony of ambivalence and indecision and every relationship a battle-ground between defiance and submission. Poised on a caricature of moral conflict, he may lose all capacity for action.

Guilt is also experienced excessively by people whose internal authority operates absolutely, prohibiting all mani-festations of those drives which require moral criteria for deciding when they are good or bad, social or anti-social. Such people believe that sex is in itself evil, or that self-assertion is always wrong, and as a result their sexual nature itself evokes guilt, quite regardless of what actions it leads them to want to perform. Their sense of guilt is further increased by the fact that their internal authority has to become progressively more severe in order to keep in check a force as protean as sex or self-assertion, while the suppressed part of their nature becomes progressively more rebellious. This again leads to an obsessional neurosis in which the patient becomes obsessed by forbidden thoughts or has to engage in all manner of rituals to prevent their emergence or to atone for them if they do. The resulting picture is a caricature of religious observances, with the neurotic sense of guilt playing the role of Original Sin, and the compulsive symptoms the roles of religious rituals and penance.

The Catholic theologian-psychiatrist Oraison has reported the case of a woman who felt compelled to go to confession five or six times a week and who experienced a dread of mortal sin in connection with such trivia as the way in which she got into a train or drank a cup of coffee. This was not a model of piety but a case of obsessional neurosis since her dread of mortal sin had nothing whatsoever to do with morality and her need for confession was a desire for magical exorcism not for forgiveness or penance. Similarly, the not uncommon impulse to blaspheme in church or do something outrageous on awe-inspiring occasions is a neurotic symptom, since it occurs in people who have no conscious hostility towards religion or ceremonial, and is in any case not a realistic or effective way of voicing scepticism or disapproval.

Neurotic guilt is not, of course, confined to the religious and it also occurs in persons who have had an entirely secular upbringing. It does, however, presuppose a division of the personality into two, a lively sense that the two are at war with one another, and an identification of the conscious self with the repressive forces of the personality and alienation from the expressive – a state of affairs perhaps most vividly describable in religious terms. The resemblance between obsessional neurosis and religious practices was the subject of an early paper by Freud in which he wrote

In view of these similarities and analogies one might venture to regard obsessional neurosis as a pathological counterpart of the formation of a religion and to describe that neurosis as an individual religiosity and religion as a universal obsessional neurosis.

The authoritarian, absolute quality of many people's internal authority derives partly from the particular nature of their upbringing and partly from the fact that the process of internalization begins at an age at which it is probably natural to think absolutely. In Freud's view intellectual precocity was an essential prerequisite for the development of an obsessional neurosis later in life. The tendency of the childhood super-ego, to use Freud's own term for the internalized authority, to operate absolutely is responsible for the fact that many adolescents experience some degree of guilt when they are adjusting their childhood values to fit the new situation created by their own maturing and by their discovery that the adult world is larger and more complex than the small sample of it that they have encountered at home and at school, and that their parents' values are likely to be to some extent outdated. This adolescent sense of guilt is a sign of health rather than illness since it indicates a capacity to tolerate conflict and face new and unfamiliar ideas and feelings. Like anxiety, which can be avoided by a phobic restriction of activity to the safe and known, guilt can be reduced by avoiding contact with new ideas. However, both manoeuvres are in the last resort life-denying and purchase freedom from guilt and anxiety at a very heavy cost. Some adolescents do nonetheless founder on issues such as what they should do about their new-found sexual potentialities or to what extent they should rebel against their parents, and typically develop an obsessional neurosis.

In the same way as adolescents may feel guilty when they begin to entertain ideas which run counter to their childhood upbringing and suffer conflict between loyalty towards the past and their attraction towards the new, so creative people may endure agonies of guilt and disloyalty before they succeed in fighting their way through to original insights. A man who had been brought up in a religious sect which

43

believed in the literal truth of the Bible and which took seriously the idea that Christianity provides a revealed set of absolute values, had several depressions, some of which required medical treatment, before he emerged in his forties as an original artist. Detailed accounts of this kind of struggle are to be found in books such as Erik Erikson's *Young Man Luther*, Edmund Gosse's *Father and Son* and Samuel Butler's *The Way of All Flesh*. The latter two show clearly that the internalized authority derives from the parents; both Gosse and Butler seem to have had a great struggle in coming to a liberal interpretation of the Fifth Commandment.

Guilt, then, seems to be the price paid by human beings for their psychological development and complexity and for their use of internalization as an adaptive device for maintaining social peace and homogeneity. It is an emotion which everyone who has reached a certain level of maturity is bound on occasion to experience and it occupies a central position in the religious thought of Western civilization. Like anxiety it may, however, become the symptom of a neurotic illness, this occurring most markedly in the case of obsessional neurosis, which seems to bear the same relation to guilt as phobia does to anxiety. It is likely to occur least in persons who have a loving nature and who do not carry a load of hostility and resentment dating from their childhood, in those whose values and temperament are compatible, and in those whose circumstances are such that they are unlikely to profit from the distress or death of those close to them. In some sections of society, such as the propertied classes and the higher reaches of the rat race, guilt may be experienced by those who know that their chance of achieving wealth and power depends on the death of employer, parent or colleague.

GUILT AND DEPRESSION

People who suffer from neurotic guilt can conveniently be divided into two groups: those who feel as though they had already committed some crime and those who feel as though they were likely to do so at any moment. Both groups experience anxiety as well as guilt, since the former behave as though they were in danger of being caught and punished and are as anxious and vigilant as an actual criminal probably is if he knows the police are on his tracks – and since the authority he fears is an internal one, it always is on his tracks – while the latter live in a state of perpetual vigilance in the hope of anticipating situations in which their forbidden impulses might find an opportunity of expressing themselves; they behave in relation to themselves like an anxious teacher, nanny, invigilator or policeman who assumes that his charge is on the point of breaking out to commit some crime. To this latter group belong not only the over-anxious and over-conscientious but also those who develop obsessional fears and have to check to make sure that they have not set their home or office on fire or have to abandon medicine because they imagine that every drug they prescribe, or every injection they give, may have contained some impurity which will kill the patient. Such people prove, on analysis, to have had personalities designed to prevent the emergence of hostility and their symptoms are a response to some recognition that, as it were, some leak has developed in their defences and that ordinary efficiency and conscientiousness are no longer sufficient to keep their hostility under control.

Those who feel as though they have already committed a crime suffer depression as well as guilt and anxiety. Indeed patients with severe depressive illnesses which require their admission to hospital to reduce the risk of suicide, often assert that they have committed some crime. Sometimes this delusional idea is expressed in a more or less plausible form and they will claim that the recent death of some relative was entirely due to their neglect or mishandling, but often it is couched in nebulous or bizarre terms: they have committed the sin against the Holy Ghost or were responsible for some recent natural disaster. Curiously enough an element of boasting can often be detected in these self-accusations. They are the most miserable sinner the world has ever known; no one has ever left a greater trail of misery behind him.

Less disturbed patients may behave in a way that would suggest they are criminals, without going to the length of actually proclaiming their guilt. A wealthy man in his thirties left his home country and came to live in London where he led a secluded life, avoiding his compatriots, failing to inform his family when he changed address, and dressing as though he were poor. He behaved as though he was on the run, but it was only in dreams that the police searched his flat and found a corpse in it: and when a compatriot did seek him out, it was only a thought in his head that this man had come to inform him that one of his relatives had been murdered. This man's crime was in his imagination and his flight was from the site of a crime which the sane part of him knew was a neurotic fantasy. Indeed his conscious motive for coming to London was to find an analyst who could rid him of feeling and behaving as though he were the Wandering Jew.

In such cases hostility and ambivalence have done more than induce guilt and anxiety. It has produced the feeling that the person one loves, or believes one ought to love, has actually been killed by one's hate. For this to happen the process of internalization must have over-reached itself, since the depressed person is treating his internal images as though they were as real as the external figures they represent, and is reacting as though the wish to kill someone was tantamount to doing so. The image has become equated with the object, and fantasy has become equated with action. This, it seems, can only happen to people in whom hate has been evoked very early in life, before the distinction between internal image and external object has become firmly established, and who have suffered some disaster in childhood which has shattered their self-confidence and confirmed for them the primitive belief that malevolent wishes are magically effective. According to Felix Brown depression occurs much more frequently in persons who have lost a parent in childhood than in the population at large.

DEPRESSION AND GRIEF

In the previous section I have described depression of the severe kind that used to be known as melancholia, and have treated it as an exacerbation or complication of neurotic guilt. Although this kind of reaction occurs most frequently in persons with obsessional tendencies, the work of Freud and Abraham has shown that it is most profitably regarded as a morbid form of grief. Grief is the emotion which occurs after bereavement and during mourning, and melancholic depression can be regarded as a form of grief in which the bereavement is an internal loss produced by the melancholic's fantasy of having destroyed some internal authority. The melancholic behaves not only as though he had lost someone but also as though he were himself responsible for this loss, and he therefore suffers not only grief but also guilt and remorse. In normal mourning it is, of course, usually obvious who or what is being mourned, but in melancholic depression there is no actual external loss and the grief therefore appears inexplicable both to the depressed person and to those around him. Sometimes it may not require much investigation to discover that some, objectively speaking, small loss or disappointment has revived the emotions appropriate to some earlier actual loss – some people always feel depressed when they have to move house – but in other cases the depression is due to the breakdown of some longstanding system of defences by which the patient has contrived to repress a deep-seated conviction that he has lost contact with all external figures and that this loss of contact is the result of his own destructiveness. Although depression appears to be a morbid state of mind which from time to time afflicts otherwise healthy people, closer scrutiny suggests that persons predisposed to depression are alienated people who have covered up the disillusioning effects of some infantile trauma by the formation of a 'false self', and that they are in fact examples of the process I described at the end of the section on infantile trauma.

It is, of course, possible for depression and grief to co-exist and, using the term in its widest sense of reduced vitality, depression is certainly an essential part of normal grief. However, pathological depression occurring after an actual loss can be distinguished from normal grief by the intensity of the remorse and guilt, which goes far beyond the sense of regret which usually accompanies grief, and by the failure of mourning to take its normal course. As we live in a society which, as Geoffrey Gorer has pointed out, increasingly regards death as unnatural and indecent and insists that mourning should be carried out in isolation and as quickly as possible, it is impossible to be precise about the normal course of mourning, but the melancholic reaction to bereavement seems to differ from normal mourning in that it prevents tears and delays the feelings of sorrow and sadness which have to be admitted before anyone can come out of mourning. In a sense indeed the melancholic reaction is a denial of grief, since it diverts the bereaved person's attention from the tragedy of the death on to the enormity of his own guilt, and from his helplessness in the face of death on to his imagined omnipotence in having caused it.

In pure grief there is a conspicuous absence of anxiety, since what was feared has in fact happened, and the agitation, anxiety and anger which often occur immediately after bereavement should be regarded as part of the struggle against admitting that the loss has irretrievably taken place. This initial phase of mourning, which Darwin called 'frantic grief' and which Bowlby calls the stage of protest, includes anxiety since there remains the lingering belief that something can still be done, though what that something is cannot be discovered. But, to quote Darwin, as soon as the sufferer is fully conscious that nothing can be done, despair or deep sorrow takes the place of frantic grief. The sufferer sits motionless, or gently rocks to and fro: the circulation becomes languid; respiration is almost forgotten, and deep sighs are drawn

a picture which is the very antithesis of anxiety.

NEUROTIC DEPRESSION

In the previous two sections I have been discussing a particular and fairly easily definable type of depression which many organically-minded psychiatrists regard as psychotic rather than neurotic and treat with anti-depressant drugs rather than by psychotherapy. However, both psychiatrists and their patients also use the word depression to describe less intense states of diminished vitality. Some of these are similar to melancholic depression and can be interpreted along the same lines but differ from it in that the hostility, guilt and ambivalence are less intense – or, alternatively, that the patient has a stronger personality which enables him to carry a heavier load of depression without breaking down. Sometimes, however, the word depression is used to describe the mood which accompanies repression, and the complaint of being depressed really refers to the feeling of being blocked by excessive inhibition. This state of being, as it were, unable to move because the foot is on the brake as well as the accelerator is, as I shall describe in detail in the next chapter, due to the activation of defences by signal-anxiety. This kind of neurotic depression needs to be distinguished from apathy, which is analogous to putting the car in neutral, a procedure which can be life-saving in situations of long-continued frustration and deprivation in which the retention of feeling would lead to impotent rage and exhaustion. According to Ralph Greenson, American soldiers in Japanese prisoner-of-war camps who became apathetic had a higher survival rate than those who continued to feel angry or hopeful. Neurotic depression may also be confused with despair, in which there is, or appears to be, a real decrease in drive and vitality, and with physical fatigue and ill-health which has yet to declare itself in specific symptoms. Apathy, despair and physiological impairment of vitality, all of which lead to depression in its widest sense, are flaccid and listless states of body and mind, in striking contrast to both melancholic and neurotic depression which are tense and agitated.

SHAME

A chapter on guilt and depression would be incomplete without a section on shame, which is often and readily confused with guilt. Theoretically speaking, shame is the Cinderella of the emotions and the literature on it is scanty. This seems to be due to the fact that psycho-analysis made its first observations on hysteria and obsessional neurosis, conditions which are characterized by anxiety and guilt rather than by shame, and which can be explained in terms of the individual's relations to his impulses and his internalized authorities without reference to his relation to himself or to the phenomenon of self-consciousness. As a result shame has been either neglected or treated as though it were a variety of guilt.

According to Helen Merell Lynd, whose *On Shame and The Search for Identity* is by far the most sensitive study of shame that we have, its obscurity derives in part from the fact that it is a private emotion which is inherently difficult to communicate, and in part from the fact that the sort of experiences which evoke it are usually nebulous and hard to define.

A particular situation [she writes], may give rise to guilt or to shame or to both. But guilt is more concerned with the codified act involved, shame with the uncodified detail and with the diffused feeling. Stealing a dime, killing a man, committing adultery ... are specific acts of guilt which can be fitted into a more or less coherent scheme and which carry recognized consequences that can, to some extent at least, be anticipated. Nothing comparable covers lack of beauty or grace, errors of taste and congruence, weakness and certain kinds of failure, feelings of meanness or envy, rejection of the gift of oneself – situations that are experienced as exposure of deeply personal inadequacy.

The *Concise Oxford Dictionary* defines shame as a 'feeling of humiliation excited by consciousness of guilt or shortcoming, of having made oneself or been made ridiculous, or having offended against propriety, modesty or decency' and it seems to arise most acutely if we are confronted unexpectedly with a discrepancy between our actual nature or behaviour and some unquestioned preconception of ourselves, and are therefore compelled to re-evaluate our self-image – or at least momentarily take cognisance of some aspect of ourselves which is incompatible with our usual self-image. Shame is usually, though not always, provoked by an exposure, either physical or mental, in front of others, and in this connection Helen Merell Lynd quotes Sartre's remark that 'the Other is the indispensable mediator between myself and me. I am ashamed of myself as I appear to the Other.' In other words, shame is an emotion aroused by seeing oneself as one imagines one is being seen by someone else and being compelled to notice that the external view of oneself does not correspond with one's illusions and wishes about oneself. Although this is most likely to occur if someone else is actually present, situations can, I think, arise in which one finds oneself playing the role of the little boy in the story of the Emperor's New Clothes to oneself as the Emperor without the mediation of someone else's physical presence.

In emphasizing the fundamental role of self-consciousness in shame Helen Merell Lynd is taking up a position subtly different from the usual psycho-analytical explanations of shame, which have tended to regard it as a fear of ridicule by others (or by one's internal authority) or as the sense of having failed to live up to some ideal which one has set oneself, explanations which resemble one another in relating shame to the response of the self to some internal agency of a higher order than itself – in analytical terminology, the super-ego and the ego-ideal, respectively. For her the essence of shame is not the feeling of having failed to achieve some goal or ideal which has already been set for one either by oneself or by an external authority, but the discovery that there are aspects of oneself and of one's relation to others of which one has been oblivious and has never subjected to self-scrutiny. As a result she holds that shame is an experience which may lead to an increase of self-knowledge and insight.

Much social embarrassment can be interpreted in this way. If one finds oneself in a situation in which one does not know the right thing to do, in which one is clearly considered to be unsuitably clothed, or in which some joke one has made or opinion one has expressed encounters unexpected disapproval or non-comprehension, one is likely to feel embarrassed and to discover that one's own standards and received opinions are not as absolute as one had imagined, and that one's own world is less of the whole world than one had previously realized. Most people, I think, can remember moments of acute shame in their adolescence when they failed to take into account the possibility that opinions and attitudes which they had adopted uncritically in their childhood turned out not to be universally acceptable in the larger world that they were entering. Such occurrences may lead to an increase of insight, provided, of course, that one does not retreat into a shell of complacency.

Shame differs from guilt in that it tends to be associated with failures to do things that one thinks one should be able to do, while guilt tends to be associated with failures to stop oneself doing things that one wants to do. Whereas guilt occurs when one fails to conform to some moral, social or religious restriction on an action that would in itself be enjoyable or advantageous, shame occurs when one fails to be as manly, assertive or intelligent as one thinks one should be. I have stated this in terms of masculine pride, since the feminine experience of shame is described in the passage from Helen Merell Lynd which I quoted above. It would seem indeed that pride and shame are the equivalents of righteousness and guilt in a value-system that puts functional capacity into the central position occupied by goodness or virtue in religious thinking, and that this shame-morality plays as dynamic a part in human psychology as does guilt-morality.

Shame and guilt are, however, identical in respect of their relation to anxiety. In the same way as the person predisposed to guilt lives in a state of perpetual vigilance in the hope of anticipating situations in which his forbidden impulses might find an outlet, so the person predisposed to shame develops social anxiety and becomes phobic about situations in which he may be compared with others, and may be compelled to compare himself with others. Alternatively he may develop a carapace, a reserve which prevents others from getting close enough to him to find out what kind of person he really is, and will become anxious if anyone makes determined efforts to get through to him. The most shame-ridden person I have ever encountered, who was intellectually pretentious, not only avoided all informal social occasions, but also refused to have his intelligence tested or to take examinations in which the successful candidates were classed or listed in order of merit. He refused, in fact, to expose his intellectual pretensions to any social evaluation.

Although shame, like guilt and anxiety, is experienced at times by everyone who has reached a certain level of self-awareness, it occurs most intensely and frequently in the so-called schizoid character, in whom it appears to play much the same role as guilt does in obsessional neurosis. Schizoid characters are persons who 'fancy themselves' and believe, consciously or unconsciously, that they possess some attribute which sets them a cut above the rest of the human race, but who half-realize that their pretensions will not be endorsed by others. They are compelled, therefore, either to become recluses who avoid situations in which their pretensions might be put to the test of comparison with others, or to divide their personalities into two, one of which conforms to society's conception of their identity while the other retains its belief in its superiority. Such people suffer the disadvantages of both self-deception and insight, since they are acutely aware of the discrepancy which exists between their private, secret image of themselves and the impression they create on others. Unlike the really gifted, who can in time compel society to accept their private images as valid, and the really insane, who can, apparently, ignore the fact that no one else believes that they are Christ or Napoleon, the shame-ridden schizoid character lacks a sense of identity in the most absolute sense; he believes he is a nonentity, but this is unendurable and so he has to pretend he is Someone. Such persons have, it seems, suffered some catastrophe in their childhood, similar but even more devastating than that suffered by the melancholic, which has shattered their belief in themselves and from which they have attempted to cure themselves by developing compensatory fantasies of their superiority.

Shame also resembles guilt in one other respect. Just as the guilty melancholic may come to believe that he has in fact committed some crime and become depressed and full of remorse, so the schizoid person may come to feel that he has shamed himself irretrievably and to suffer mortification. And the feeling that no reparation is possible may lead both to commit suicide.

Chapter 4

Inhibitions, Symptoms
and Anxiety

In the three previous chapters I have discussed the general
nature of anxiety and its relationship to other basic emotions
such as fear, concern, fright, shock, guilt, depression and
shame. I have argued that anxiety is not in itself a pathological or neurotic phenomenon but I have, I hope, made it clear
that it often is, and that one form of anxiety, signal-anxiety,
is evoked by the stirring of unconscious, repressed mental
activity to which the individual reacts as though it were a
threat from outside himself. I have not, however, yet discussed in any detail the role of anxiety in neurosis, nor
indeed have I explained precisely what I mean by this word,
despite having given some account of a number of neurotic
states.

The purpose of this present chapter is to remedy these
omissions. I have borrowed its title from the work by Freud
in which he formulated the concept of signal-anxiety, since
the three terms, inhibition, symptom and anxiety, can be
used both to define neurosis and to elucidate its general
structure. Although, as I shall explain in the next chapter,
satisfactory accounts of particular neuroses require that the
concept of inhibition be broken down into a number of

specific defences, the account given by Freud in his *Inhibitions, Symptoms and Anxiety* of the general nature of neurosis remains the simplest and most convenient that we have. It is also the formulation which corresponds best with medical habits of thought.

NEUROSIS DEFINED

A neurosis may be defined as a condition occurring in an otherwise healthy person which is characterized by the presence of both anxiety and other symptoms – these other symptoms being explicable in terms of a conflict between inhibiting and inhibited parts of the personality. The one exception to this definition is the traumatic neurosis proper which I discussed in Chapter 2.

The proviso 'occurring in an otherwise healthy person' is necessary for a number of reasons. Firstly, neurosis is by definition a condition not attributable to physical illness and it occurs in people who are demonstrably in good physical health. Even if the symptoms are apparently physical, they can be shown to correspond to the patient's idea of how his body works and not to the physiological and anatomical facts. In Graves's Disease (thyrotoxicosis) the patient suffers from both anxiety and other symptoms, but this is not a neurosis since clinical examination shows that the patient has a lump in his neck and biochemical tests show that his thyroid gland is overactive. In hysteria, on the other hand, the patient may also complain of anxiety and of a lump in his neck, but this is a neurosis, since the lump turns out to be due to the tightening of the throat muscles which occurs in anxiety and biochemical tests show that his thyroid gland is functioning normally. In the former case, the anxiety is due to the fact that one of the endocrine glands responsible for maintaining physiological vigilance has become overactive, while in the latter it is due to some psychological factor which can only be elucidated by psychotherapy. Similarly, anaesthesia of the hands occurs in a number of neurological diseases and also in hysteria, but in the latter the area of numbness corrsponds to the concept 'hand' and not to the areas of skin served by particular sensory nerves. I am not, of course, maintaining that it is impossible for a person to have a physical illness and a neurosis at the same time but that the two conditions are distinct. I remember as a medical student being very impressed by a man who complained that his congenitally deformed and almost useless right hand had become paralysed. But the paralysis did not fit his anatomy; it was hysterical and had developed shortly after the death of his mother who had inevitably been a right hand to him.

The assertion that neurotic symptoms are demonstrably not attributable to physical causes implies, of course, that reasonable certainty exists as to how the body works. One of the historical prerequisites for the emergence of psychological theories of neurosis at the end of the nineteenth century was the fact that medicine, and in particular neurology, had become sufficiently advanced to be able to distinguish between 'organic' illnesses, in which it was possible to locate the site and nature of the physical lesion, and 'functional' illnesses, in which no physical lesion could be discovered either in life or at *post mortem*. These functional illnesses were at first thought to be physiological disturbances of function which did not produce organic changes, but since Freud there has been very little attempt to explain neuroses, even by those who are antagonistic to his specific theories, in terms of hypothetical but invisible lesions of the nervous system, and the idea that they should be regarded as manifestations of psychological and emotional conflict has become generally accepted. Since Freud was not only a physician but also a neurologist and an expert on brain anatomy, he was, incidentally, well placed to be sceptical of the idea that the neuroses might be due to some as yet undiscovered lesion in the brain or elsewhere.

Another reason for qualifying my definition of neurosis is

that a neurosis can only occur in persons who are otherwise in good mental health. For historical reasons which it would be tedious to elucidate, psychiatrists use the word 'psychosis' to refer to those mental illnesses which so affect the whole personality that the patient may have to be regarded as insane, and 'neurosis' to refer to those in which the personality remains intact; this despite the fact that some of the psychoses are undoubtedly physical in origin, and that no one now believes that the neuroses are in any sense diseases of the nervous system. As a result of this terminology, a neurosis is by definition a condition in which the patient is neither psychotic nor insane.

To be even more precise, the neuroses only occur in persons who are not only sane but also basically normal – in the sense that their sexual inclinations are heterosexual and linked with the idea of love, and that they internalize parental figures and develop consciences. Although the word 'neurotic' has come to be used loosely to refer to anyone whose troubles can be regarded as psychological and is often applied to perverts, addicts and persons suffering from the so-called 'behaviour-disorders', strict medical and psychiatric terminology restricts the term neurosis to four conditions: anxiety-neurosis, phobias, obsessional neurosis and hysteria, the symptoms of all of which are no more than exaggerated versions of feelings and behaviour with which every normal person is familiar. Whereas psychotics go through experiences with which only exceptionally imaginative people can identify, and perverts and persons with personality-disorders engage in actions which disgust or shock, neurotics suffer from symptoms with which the normal person can sympathize easily and from which he has at times himself suffered – if not in the present as an adult, at least in the past as a child. The extension of the term 'neurotic' to include the behaviour-disorders seems to derive from the fact that they resemble the neuroses in being amenable to psychological explanation – though not as a rule to psychological treatment – and that their disordered behaviour resembles the fantasies (though not the actions) of neurotics. Freud indeed once remarked that the perversions were the negative of neuroses, since perverts acted on impulses which neurotics repress. The crucial difference between behaviour-disorder and neurosis seems to be that whereas the normal person deals with unacceptable impulses by selective inhibition (conscious suppression) and the neurotic deals with them by massive inhibition, persons with personality disorders deal with tension by indiscriminate action. They 'act out', as the psycho-analytical jargon has it.

Neurosis must also, in principle, be distinguished from what psycho-analysts call character-neurosis. The idea underlying character-neurosis is that a person can develop general traits of character *in lieu* of symptoms, so that instead of developing obsessional rituals or suffering from obsessional indecision, a person may develop an obsessional character and become a highly controlled, orderly and unemotional person. Such a person is not ordinarily regarded as ill and he may indeed be much admired for his strength of character, but he and his relatives may also complain that he lacks spontaneity, warmth and adaptability. Such persons rarely consult psychiatrists as patients, but are often very drawn towards psychology or psycho-analysis, since they believe that it will increase their capacity for self-control.

ANXIETY AND INHIBITION

The relationship existing in neurosis between anxiety and inhibition has already been implied in earlier sections. Some unacceptable impulse, or some painful memory, has been evoked and the self reacts to this threat to its equanimity with signal-anxiety. Alerted to the possibility of being overcome by the impulse, or of having to re-experience the painful memory, the self reacts with the same vigilance as it would to some unexpected external danger. It then deals with the impulse or memory by an increase in inhibition or repression.

As a result of this inhibition, some feeling or recollection which might have become conscious is prevented from doing so and peace of mind is purchased at the cost of impoverishment of the personality, since the effect of repression is to render parts of the whole potential self inaccessible to the conscious self. Most neurotics have a poor memory of their childhood or of certain stretches of it which not only diminishes their sense of their own continuity of being but also impairs their ability to respond imaginatively to children who are at the age corresponding to their own amnesia.* These repressed parts of the self do not become frozen but retain the expressive dynamic of all living structures and actively strive to break through the barriers which the ego has set up against them and which it has to continue to do work to maintain. Although this assumption implies the existence of, as it were, active but unconscious sub-personalities striving for self-realization, it is necessary if one is to explain neurotic symptom-formation.

SYMPTOM-FORMATION

After repression of unacceptable feelings or recollections has occurred, the process of neurosis-formation may – appar-

---

* Of recent years it has become fashionable to use words such as alienation, dissociation and splitting to describe the disruption of the personality into disconnected parts which follows repression, alienation referring to the subjective sense of being out of touch with the instinctive and emotional core of one's being, dissociation referring to the fact that the disconnected parts of the personality operate and develop independently of one another, so that the fantasy life of day-and night-dreams drains energy away from real life instead of imaginatively enriching it, and splitting referring to the fragmentation of the original unitary self. These three terms differ from inhibition and repression in that they simply describe some of the consequences of the fact that one part of the neurotic mind has no knowledge of what is going on in another part, whereas inhibition and repression refer to the fact that the conscious self or ego has to do work keeping the repressed out of consciousness.

ently at least – stop. The result is a person who is stable and free of neurotic anxiety but inhibited, and whose health is contingent on his remaining limited and incapable of realizing his full potentialities – and on his successfully avoiding situations which might upset his equilibrium. In practice, of course, it is not always easy to decide whether any particular person is inhibited or merely lacking in abilities or vitality, and many incapacities which psychotherapists tend to regard as inhibitions pass in ordinary life for idiosyncrasies which do not require an explanation and which are accepted as regrettable but inevitable defects. Clumsiness, being hopeless at games or mathematics, being totally unmusical or having no sense of direction, are all disabilities which are rarely regarded as neurotic symptoms but which may on occasion prove to be due to inhibition and vanish, either during psychotherapy or after some releasing emotional experience. A woman in her twenties found herself singing in tune for the first time after her first sexual experience.

It must be added in parentheses that the idea that lack of talent is due to inhibition is both seductive and treacherous; seductive, because it can be used to argue that we could all be geniuses if we had our inhibitions analysed away, and treacherous because it confuses general abilities with special aptitudes. Although it is, apparently, exceptional for lack of musical appreciation to be due to tone-deafness and the literature contains accounts of patients who regained the capacity to enjoy music during psycho-analysis, the evidence is overwhelmingly in favour of the idea that creative musical ability is a special aptitude which no amount of psychotherapy could instil. An extreme instance of the view that we could all be creative if our inhibitions were removed is provided by the American analyst Lawrence Kubie who in his *Neurotic Distortion of the Creative Process* refers to 'the cultural sterility and impotence of great art, literature, music and science' and argues that if man can learn to free his creative processes from neurotic distortion 'he will stand at the frontiers of wholly new lands of Canaan.'

A common symptom which is often due to inhibition is chronic fatigue. Here again it may not always be easy to decide whether someone is suffering from neurotic fatigue or is genuinely tired, and it may only be psychotherapy, or some spontaneous emotional crisis, which enables a person to discover that his fatigue was due to his excessive expenditure of energy maintaining his internal *status quo*. The great access of energy which most people enjoy when in love is due to a decrease in inhibition and the release of energy previously contained in fantasy, and many people are familiar with the increase in energy which occurs when it ceases to be necessary to suppress irritation and anger.

Some, but not all, headaches have a similar origin. This is exemplified by the story of the young man who complained to his doctor of persistent headache. After eliciting that the young man never went out with girls, never smoked or drank or went to the cinema, the doctor remarked 'I know what your trouble is. Your halo's too tight.'

However, although some neurotic symptoms can be regarded simply as manifestations of inhibition, others are due to what Freud called 'the return of the repressed'. According to Horace 'Though you drive Nature out with a pitchfork, she will still find her way back' and neurotic symptom-formation is essentially a process by which the repressed achieves its way back, usually either in disguise or by establishing some link with a part of the repressing self which enables a compromise between the repressed and the repressing forces to occur – the sudden irruption of an undisguised, unmodified repressed impulse, or the sudden total recall of a traumatic memory usually only occurs in psychosis or nightmares and constitutes a complete failure of signal-anxiety. The forms of disguise and compromise which are used depend on the precise repressed and repressing forces at work in any particular case, and on the types of defence habitually used by him, but the following examples will give some indication of what is meant by the 'return of the repressed'.

First, the unconscious impulse may become conscious but without affording any satisfaction. A man began to have the unpleasant feeling that everyone was always staring at him. He was not a shy or retiring person and had recently had a certain amount of publicity in his role of spokesman for a public body. In psychotherapy he clearly enjoyed the position of being the centre of attention and of being able to hold forth to a captive audience – even though it was only of one. It soon became clear that the idea of being looked at and of being the centre of attention was in itself enjoyable to him, but that he believed it to be a pleasure only permitted to women; he had been the fatherless son of an eccentric and domineering mother. Shortly before stopping psychotherapy he announced his intention of taking a course in elocution and going into politics. The wish to show off had become permissible and could be satisfied directly and not by developing a distressing symptom.

Secondly, the repressed impulse may return in a disguised or symbolic form which enables it, as it were, to pass the censor. For instance both children and adults with a conflict about masturbation may cease actual masturbation and instead develop habits such as fidgeting, nose-picking or scratching themselves which express the masturbatory preoccupation with their own bodies but do not incur the moral disapproval of their internalized authority. These habits may fulfil the further function of irritating others without being voluntary or deliberate; they can therefore act as vehicles for an unconscious defiance of authority. It is in general true of neurotic symptoms that their involuntary nature enables sexual, aggressive, defiant and cussed tendencies to be expressed without either conscious guilt or the risk of provoking the retaliation of others. Obsessional patients who develop washing rituals which keep them in the bathroom for hours not only derive sexual pleasure from the minute attention they pay to their own body and a feeling of virtue from their scrupulous cleanliness but also succeed in causing great inconvenience to the rest of their family.

Thirdly, the symptom may allow the repressed tendency to be satisfied without revealing what it is. Agoraphobics, patients who are afraid of venturing into strange and unfamiliar places, are mother-fixated and only feel at ease in the protective atmosphere of home. Their symptom, anxiety away from home or apart from their mother or mother-figure, enables them to stay at home, but the reason they give for staying there is not that they want to, but that they feel anxious when travelling. Consciously, they feel themselves to be adult, independent persons, and it is only their inexplicable symptom which prevents them from being as self-reliant and enterprising as the next man.

Fourthly, the unconscious tendency may become conscious but may not be recognized as being a part of the self. This leads to the well-known phenomenon of people who exemplify the parable of the mote and the beam and who are obsessively preoccupied with the vices and failings of others but who are oblivious of the fact that they have the same failings too. To this class belong the sexually inhibited who become prurient and censorious about the sex lives of others and who confirm Wilde's aphorism that to the pure all things are impure; the over-gentle who become obsessed with the problem of violence; and even the dedicated therapists, missionaries and clergy, who see clearly that others need help and sustenance but who fail to recognize their own needs and lay themselves open to the injunction 'Physician, heal thyself'. Such individuals use the defence known as projection which enables them to locate their own repressed wishes in the outside world, where they may either, as in the case of the censorious, continue their struggle against them, or as in the case of the dedicated, identify with them and extend a compassion towards others which they never grant themselves.

Phobias of specific objects and situations are often explicable in terms of projection. The situation which must never be encountered, the object which must never be seen or touched, has become the symbol of some aspect of themselves or of some part of their body from which they have become alienated. They then become ambivalent, on the one hand being obsessed and fascinated, and on the other frightened and repelled. A person who suffers from a train-phobia must be fascinated by the idea of some violent encounter for him to assume that a train accident will occur on just the day that he is travelling. Similarly, the person who has a horror of touching snakes, cats or birds is attaching some symbolic significance to such creatures which makes him both fearful of them and yet in a way anxious to get to grips with them. It is probably not an accident that all the objects and situations which evoke anxiety in phobic patients are ones which can provide intense pleasure to others. Some people delight in wide open spaces or in flying solo, or are thrilled by thunder-storms, or become enthusiastic pot-holers, train-spotters or bird-watchers.

THE PSYCHOPATHOLOGY OF EVERYDAY LIFE

The incidence of neurosis would probably be even greater than it is if it were not for the existence of various social conventions which enable inhibitions to be relaxed temporarily and to allow behaviour which is, in principle, neurotic to pass unrecognized. These conventions allow a certain leakage of repressed tendencies to occur, thereby reducing the internal pressure.

Two obvious examples of such conventions are the use of alcohol and humour. It has been said facetiously that the superego is that part of the psyche which is soluble in alcohol, and the use of alcohol as a social lubricant depends on the fact that it weakens inhibitions sooner than it impairs functions. As a result many people enjoy a sense of enhanced vitality and freedom after a few drinks which enables them to do and say things of which they would be incapable when sober. Although this enables shy and inhibited people to open out, it is not, of course, an umixed blessing. Inhibition affects not only warm-hearted social impulses but also destructive ones, and although some people become nicer when under the influence others become vicious. In addition, inhibition may mask not only anxiety but also depression, and in persons of whom this is true alcohol has a paradoxical effect; instead of releasing them it makes them depressed, morose and maudlin.

The other factor which limits the efficacy of alcohol as a therapeutic agent is that it eventually impairs functions. As a result the drunk person is not only likely to become amorous or aggressive on less provocation than he would when sober, but his performance in both ranges of activity is likely to become incompetent – and, in the case of aggressive activities like driving cars fast, dangerous. The fact that alcohol is not only intoxicating but toxic in large doses precludes its recommendation as the ideal tranquillizer, though some of the drugs which are prescribed ceremoniously and not taken spontaneously resemble alcohol chemically – and they too have their unfortunate side-effects. Alcohol nonetheless plays a very helpful role in the lives of many tense and inhibited people.

Ever since Freud wrote his *Jokes and their Relation to the Unconscious* it has been well known that humour can enable both the joker and his audience to ventilate feelings and wishes that they would not venture to express or act on seriously. Although Freud's theory that jokes are a means of expressing repressed wishes does not explain all jokes – some, like puns, seem to depend solely on incongruity, while others seem to be an elliptical way of expressing truths which it would be tedious to spell out in detail – there is certainly a number of *genres* of humour which seem to derive their popularity from enabling the repressed, taboo side of ambivalent relationships to be expressed in a way that does not count socially. Music-hall jokes about mothers-in-law and women drivers are not often witty but they circulate in a way that enables men's hostility towards women and their fear of being dominated by them to be ventilated in a way that avoids domestic strife. Obscene jokes and dirty stories perform a similar function and seem to circulate more rapidly among conventional people than among the emancipated, and among men whose conscious attitude towards women includes an element of reverence than among women themselves. They knock Woman off her pedestal – and the mystery of Sex off its – in a way that enables the joker to avoid having to take seriously the possibility that he may still be partly in awe of women. Fear and envy of authority, whether it is religious, political or intellectual, also probably lies behind more sophisticated jokes such as 'When Freud died and approached the gates of Heaven he was welcomed eagerly by St Peter who said "Thank heavens you've come; God's gone mad and thinks he's Hitler".'

Society also provides neurosis a certain lee-way by conspiring not to notice or take seriously various phenomena which psychotherapists regard as indicative of conflict and which they use daily in their work with patients. These phenomena include dreams, the slips of the tongue and other faulty actions which Freud described in his *The Psychopathology of Everyday Life*. Although psychotherapists take seriously the idea that dreams, slips, mannerisms and accidents are all significant expressions of their creators and that valid deductions can be drawn from them, the conventional attitude is that they are trivia best not noticed, that dreams are meaningless, that mannerisms are just idiosyncracies, and that slips of the tongue and faulty actions are merely accidental. As a result, people who can never remember names other than their own are not charged with egotism, women

67

who have a trick of fidgeting with their wedding ring are not compelled to face the possibility that they have a marital problem, and the perpetrators of slips of the tongue are not required to spell out in detail the full implications of what they actually said. Although this conspiracy of obtuseness allows a lot of hypocrisy to pass unexposed, it also enables many people to survive without having to face up to conflicts with which they might not be able to cope without expert assistance – which in view of the shortage of psychotherapists is probably fortunate. It is also responsible for the fact that, as Geoffrey Gorer has remarked, very few people feel at ease in the presence of a psycho-analyst.

Chapter 5

Defence and Adaptive Behaviour

In the previous chapter I outlined the general structure of a neurosis, which I conceived as being the result of conflict between repressing and repressed parts of the personality, the tendency of the latter to force itself back into consciousness leading to neurotic anxiety, increased inhibition and the development of symptoms. My account was based largely on Freud's *Inhibitions, Symptoms and Anxiety* and it includes two assumptions which merit discussion.

Firstly, it assumes a tendency for the personality to divide into two parts, a controlling ego concerned with maintaining its own stability and an impulsive id striving for self-expression. On this assumption neurosis is an indication either that the neurotic has stronger or more dangerous impulses than others, which makes it harder for him to control them or, alternatively, that he has a weaker ego which makes return of the repressed more likely – the strength of the impulses and the stability of the ego being dependent on either constitutional or developmental factors. Psycho-analysis has become popularly associated with explanation in terms of childhood environmental influences, but Freud himself was often inclined to constitutional explanations and he thought it

possible that obsessional neurosis, the condition to which
the signal-anxiety theory of neurosis applies most aptly, was
due either to an innate excess of sadism or to inherent
precocity of the ego, which led the future neurotic to repress
in infancy and childhood impulses which the healthy child
expresses freely. In either case this theory assumes that the
neurotic is suffering from the effect of a back-log of childhood impulses which in adult life are still craving for
expression and which overtax his capacity to manage his
adult emotions. His wife becomes the object not only of the
conscious adult emotions which she evokes in her own right
but also of unconscious feelings which derive from his
childhood relationship with his mother; and his employer is
similarly the object of emotions which historically belong to
his father. According to this view the neurotic is a person for
whom childhood is not over and done with and whose
capacity to deal with the stresses of adult life is impaired by
his having simultaneously to cope with the residue of
childhood conflict. He is, therefore, likely to break down or
develop symptoms at a lower intensity of strain and unhappiness than the person whose fortunate constitution or childhood does not require him to waste his energies in a struggle
with repressed parts of himself.

Secondly, the theory that neurosis is the result of a conflict
between a controlling ego and an impulsive id takes the nature
of the ego for granted. As I, and others, have argued elsewhere, classical Freudian theory tends to assume that the
ego is intrinsically anti-emotional and anti-instinctual and
that it inevitably feels threatened by anything which disturbs
its objectivity, equanimity and consciousness of self. However, this 'theoretical ideal of rational action', to quote a
phrase of Heinz Hartmann, the leading exponent of psycho-
analytical ego-psychology, which leads to the tendency to
react defensively to all irrational feeling, appears not to be a
universal characteristic of the human ego but to be confined
to Western civilization and, in particular, to its educated

classes. In other societies, in which the detached, scientific attitude and its moral counterpart, the ever-judging conscience, are not part of the inculcated tradition, there seems to be much less fear of emotions or of states of mind like trances which temporarily overthrow self-consciousness. According to Professor Lambo, neurosis, depression and suicide are rarer among un-Westernized West Africans than they are among Europeans – though murder and short-lived delusional states are commoner.

In a recent article in *The Listener* Professor Carstairs described how a widow in the Hindu village of Delwara used to go into trances in which speaking in a deep voice she gave her dead husband's instructions for the management of his affairs.

From the outsider's point of view, it was obvious that only in this way was she able to exercise real authority in the household; but there was no question of simulation – when the moment came, she simply surrendered to the state of trance.

Although in our culture the widow often retains a living image of her dead husband and tries to run his affairs as he would have, such total recall while awake would almost certainly arouse intense anxiety in a Western woman and be regarded as a psychiatric emergency by her relatives.

Unless, therefore, one takes the arrogant view that the Western ego alone is normal and that members of other societies and civilizations are primitive or deviant, one has to admit that neurosis is a relative phenomenon which depends largely on the type of ego which any particular society regards as normal, and that the forms of neurosis with which we in this country are familiar are, in part at least, the price we pay for setting a high value on self-discipline, on moral and intellectual consistency, and on remaining self-aware and objective.

DEFENCE

Recognition that it is not possible to explain neurotic phenomena solely in terms of what is repressed has led to the development of ego-psychology, in which the emphasis is not merely on the symptom and what it expresses and symbolizes, but also on the various techniques used by the ego when it is alerted by signal-anxiety. Instead of assuming that the ego has only one way of dealing with unacceptable feelings, that of rendering them unconscious and keeping them so, it is assumed that it has a variety of techniques. This change in theoretical orientation was foreshadowed by Freud in an appendix to his *Inhibitions, Symptoms and Anxiety* in which he wrote

It will be an undoubted advantage, I think, to revert to the old concept of 'defence', provided we employ it explicitly as a general designation for all the techniques which the ego makes use of in conflicts which may lead to a neurosis, while we retain the word 'repression' for the special method of defence which the line of approach taken by our investigations made us better acquainted with in the first instance.

These techniques are usually called defence-mechanisms, though the term defence is really preferable since it does not carry the implication that defences operate mechanically nor that their use is always automatic and unconscious. Defences are better regarded less as mechanisms than as techniques, manoeuvres, strategies or ploys, all terms which are as applicable to active mastery of external and internal threats as to passive resistance of the kind exemplified by repression proper. Although the psychological concept defence refers in the first instance to techniques for dealing with internal threats, it seems legitimate to extend it to include techniques for dealing with external situations which evoke objective anxiety, particularly as psycho-analytical theory has always assumed that the ego responds similarly to the outside world and to those parts of itself from which it has become alienated. As Anna Freud has put it, 'The defensive methods . . . are motivated by the three principal types of anxiety to which the ego is exposed – instinctual anxiety, objective anxiety and anxiety of conscience.' This extension makes it possible to correlate defences with certain biological patterns of adaptive behaviour.

Although the concept defence is used by analysts of all schools, considerable disagreement exists both as to the number of defences and as to how they should be classified. Anna Freud adopts the method of enumeration and lists ten specific defence-mechanisms, while Fairbairn,* in his 'A Revised Psychopathology of the Psychoses and Psychoneuroses', described four general techniques, but although both Anna Freud and Fairbairn correlate their mechanisms and techniques with specific neuroses, it is not possible to reconcile the two classificatory systems by, for instance, dividing Anna Freud's ten specific mechanisms into four groups which correspond to Fairbairn's general techniques. The reason for this is that they make different assumptions about what is being defended against. In Anna Freud's view it is anxiety provoked by threats to mental equilibrium, while in Fairbairn's it is anxiety provoked by the threat of losing the sense of security provided by the originally non-ambivalent relationship with the mother. As a result they also differ in their view of the function of defence. For Anna

* W. R. D. Fairbairn (1889–1964) was a pioneer exponent of object-relations theory, which re-states psycho-analytical theory in terms of the individual's need to maintain contact with an object, as opposed to the instinct-theory of Freud which centres round the need to find instinctual satisfaction. He held that man is inherently object-seeking not pleasure-seeking and that the neuroses are the result of attempts to control and reduce ambivalence towards the object, who is originally (and, unconsciously, always) the mother, by means of four basic defensive manoeuvres, which he called the schizoid, hysterical, phobic and obsessional techniques. In Fairbairn's own formulations these defensive techniques are distinguished by differences in the way in which the object is internalized, but in what follows I have made no attempt to discuss to what extent my exposition is, or is not, compatible with his general theory of neurosis.

Freud it is to prevent the ego being overwhelmed, whereas for Fairbairn it is to maintain the illusion that there still exists an ideal mother and to divert aggression from this ideal image. And both are thinking solely of anxiety as a neurotic phenomenon and not of its wider connection with biology.

If, however, one takes the view which I have adopted throughout this book, and regards anxiety as a form of vigilance which can be evoked by changes in both the external environment and in those parts of the self which the ego treats as though they were external, it becomes possible to classify defences by relating them to biological adaptive responses.

As we have already seen, both animals and human beings become alert and vigilant when they perceive something new in their environment. This vigilance prepares them for action, and does so before they are in a position to decide what form the action should take. If the newly perceived object turns out to be dangerous or threatening, three different types of self-protective response are available, attack, flight and submission, the last being the response of a weaker animal to the threatening behaviour of a more dominant member of its own species. I am here suggesting that psychological defences are analogous to these three forms of biological response, which they resemble in being preceded by anxiety and in being designed to preserve the individual's integrity. They differ, however, from them in that they are designed more to preserve his psychological integrity than to ensure his physical survival. One of the consequences of the greater psychological development of human beings and of their self-consciousness is that they guard their psychological integrity as vigilantly as animals do their physical integrity and are capable of feeling hurt, deprived, threatened or insecure as a result of purely mental changes in their environment. There is, indeed, evidence that the physical responses of human beings to psychological stress may resemble those of animals to physical danger. According to S. A. Barnett,

In man, increased adrenal cortical secretion occurs during disagreeable experiences with other people as well as emergencies which threaten injury or death: evidently, the bodily response to humiliation resembles, in some ways, that to danger to life or limb.

Psychological defences also differ from biological response to physical emergencies in that they are affected and complicated by the process of internalization which I described in Chapter 3. Instead of attacking or fleeing from situations or persons who threaten their psychological integrity, human beings may submit to the overpowering agency and then internalize it. Thereafter, the responses of attack, flight and submission relate not to actual environmental figures but to their internal mental representations, and the individual is engaged in purely psychological conflict with his environment. The long childhood of human beings enhances this tendency to internalization, but the same process may occur in adults if they are trapped in a concentration camp or a totalitarian country.

As a result of these two factors, human psychological defences are more complex than the responses of animals to danger and they operate more at the level of symbolic thought than that of physical reaction. I shall, nonetheless, attempt in the succeeding sections of this chapter to show that the four defensive techniques described by Fairbairn and termed by him the obsessional, phobic, schizoid and hysterical defences, are psychological elaborations of the biological responses, attack, flight and submission.

ATTACK AND THE OBSESSIONAL DEFENCE

Attack is well known to be the best form of defence, and to decrease anxiety by mastering its cause is not, of course, a neurotic defence. On the contrary, healthy growth consists to a large extent of a progressive mastery of situations and people who initially arouse anxiety. I am here referring not only to the increasingly complex external environment, populated by an increasing number of unfamiliar and possibly hostile people, which we encounter as we proceed from infancy to childhood, and from childhood to adulthood, but also to the biological changes which occur in ourselves. For persons whose habitual response is mastery, anxiety goes hand-in-hand with curiosity and expectation, and growing-up is not just a painful feeling of being expelled from what is in fact the largely illusory security of childhood but is also a process of discovering new opportunities in the outside world and new capacities in oneself. In Chapter 1 I quoted Pavlov on the what-is-it? reflex, which in one way is a defence without which life would at every moment hang by a thread, but which is also the basis of curiosity, and of the capacity to make exploration of the unknown an adventure. The same principle applies even to neurotic phenomena. The person who suffers from nightmares and becomes curious about their cause and meaning is attacking the problem with which some residual childhood conflict has confronted him, and his response to his neurosis is not in itself neurotic. The neurotic who seeks help in psychotherapy may or may not be using the response of attack, but if he uses therapy to increase his self-understanding he is, since he is trying to get on top of his problems. If, on the other hand, he seeks protection and guidance from his therapist, he compounds his original neurosis by adding to it the neurotic response of submission to authority.

That mastery can be used as a defence against not only objective anxiety induced by situations which really give grounds for fear, but also against subjective or neurotic anxiety, is shown by the fact that children not uncommonly dare one another (and themselves) to perform acts which make them anxious but which they nonetheless realize or believe are feasible. In this way they both invoke pride and self-respect to help them overcome an anxiety which they recognize to be unfounded and acquire valuable experience about the precise nature of physical hazards – and about their own capacity to tolerate anxiety.

There is, however, a form of attack or mastery which must certainly be accounted neurotic. This is the compulsion to control everyone and everything which is characteristic of those who are liable to develop obsessional neurosis. Whereas healthy persons engage in spontaneous relationships in which they allow free interplay of emotions between themselves and others, expressing and receiving affection and anger without anxiety, obsessional characters attempt to control their emotions and to pin down both themselves and others in predetermined positions and attitudes. In this way they hope to avoid anxiety by eliminating the unpredictable element in human relationships. If they can attain self-control to the extent of never being overcome by an unexpected emotion and can control others so that they cease to be free agents capable of spontaneous and therefore unexpected actions, then, according to the logic of the obsessional defence, the unexpected will never happen and the unknown will never be encountered – and anxiety will never arise. Since, however, emotions are by their very nature spontaneous, unpredictable and unwillable, the obsessional defence leads to antagonism towards emotion as such, and feelings come to be regarded as intruders which disturb the orderliness of the world of which the obsessional has made himself master. As a result, the person who uses obsessional defences tends to adopt an attitude towards both his own emotional self and the emotional lives of others which is reminiscent of a bureaucrat who administers an alien and potentially hostile population. He regards his own impulses and those of others with circumspection, if not suspicion; he is easily disturbed by changes in routine and prefers to concentrate on the formal and ritualistic aspects of personal relationships than on the intimate and subjective, since the former can be codified and predicted while the latter elude classification. Confronted with the prospect of marriage, the person who uses obsessional defences will pay enormous attention to the details of the marriage ceremony, to whatever financial settlements may be necessary, to the purchase of the marital home, and to the taking out of life-insurance policies, since these are all activities which enable a step into the unknown to be dealt with as though it were an intellectual exercise in the administration and re-organization of already familiar entities. In emancipated circles, this need to control and anticipate the unknown will lead the husband-to-be to purchase books on Harmony in Marriage so that even the mysteries of sex may be controlled by being converted into a problem in technology.

Obsessional characters are often attracted to psychology, since it seems to hold out the possibility of knowing about and therefore being able to control precisely those aspects of themselves and others which are most elusive and unpredictable. They find psychological theories which ignore intuition, which rely on statistical analyses, and which include the idea or ideal of 'normality', particularly fascinating, since they encourage the notion that emotions can be mastered intellectually and that there is a known and desirable pattern of behaviour to which one can adjust oneself – thereby enabling them to feel that it is always possible to tread on safe and familiar territory.

They are also attracted by philosophical systems since they create the illusion that it might be possible to discover a key to the universe which would enable one to understand everything in general and thus to become immune to anxiety-provoking encounters with unknown particulars.

On a more mundane level, the obsessional need to control everything leads to a preoccupation with orderliness and tidiness, which are valued not so much because they are aids to efficiency as because there is a sense of power in knowing where everything is – and a sense of anxiety attaching to disorder, since it means either that objects are, as it were, in revolt or, alternatively, that someone else has been encroaching on one's territory.

This need to control contributes towards the obsessional tendency to internalize excessively. Although persons and things in the outer world are only to a limited extent in one's power, words and thoughts can be manipulated without any risk that they will refuse to cooperate, and the internalizing shift from external objects on to their mental and verbal representations enables the obsessional to acquire the illusion of mastery over a much larger world than can really be controlled. Although it is impossible to know or control every country in the world, it is possible to know the name of every country and to decide whether one shall list them alphabetically, or in order of size or importance.

The obsessional defence consists then in an attempt to deal with the anxiety which is inherent in all human relationships by treating all spontaneous tendencies, whether in oneself or others, as though they were dangerous invaders of a territory of which one had acquired absolute power and knowledge, and then adopting the same defence towards these invaders as animals use when their territory is literally invaded, *viz*. attack in an attempt to expel the intruder or force him into submission. When the intruder is really an alienated part of the self, the response of attack manifests itself as repression; when it is spontaneous behaviour of others, it leads to attempts to control and dominate them and to deny their reality as free agents. When obsessional characters start psycho-analytical treatment they regularly inform themselves of every available detail of analytical theory and technique, and become indignant and aggressively anxious if their analyst says or does anything which does not conform with *their* view of how the analysis should be conducted.

Despite its efficiency as a defence, both forms of obsessional attack, the inwardly-directed repression and the outwardly-directed control, are ultimately self-defeating since they purchase freedom from anxiety at the price of loss of spontaneity and of alienation from the life of the emotions. In *Words*, the first volume of his autobiography, J.-P. Sartre, the apostle of alienation, gives a clear and ironically amusing account of the way in which, as a child, the discovery of words gave him a sense of power over a world from which he felt himself entirely divorced, and of how his habit of adopting self-conscious poses prevented him acquiring any real self-knowledge. Not surprisingly, this volume had a disturbing effect on those who had been persuaded by his earlier writings that *angoisse* and alienation were inevitable concomitants of the human condition.

In preceding paragraphs I have more than once used the metaphor of territory being mastered or invaded. Although this metaphor came to my mind solely as a descriptive device, it is, I think, possible that there is a real connection between the obsessional defence and the phenomenon of territoriality in animals. In many species of animals the males establish an area of their own into which other males are not admitted and which they guard vigilantly. Should another male enter his territory, the occupying male attacks him, forcing him into either flight or submission. Obsessional defence – and neurosis – is markedly more common in men than in women and it is tempting to see it as a symbolic version, or rather perversion, of the mastery of their physical environment practised by male animals.

FLIGHT AND THE PHOBIC AND SCHIZOID DEFENCES

The function of flight is to put oneself at a distance from danger. Among animals it is evoked typically by threatening behaviour on the part of an obviously stronger member of one's own species or by the presence of a predator of whom one is the natural prey. In human beings use of this defence is obviously not always neurotic, since it may be based on a realistic assessment of one's physical or psychological weakness in the face of either physical danger or persons who are more powerful than oneself, whether by reason of their physical strength or their superior status.

The simplest example of neurotic flight is provided by the phobic defence. Persons who use this defence habitually avoid situations which make them anxious. They run away from them and attempt to organize their lives in a way that will ensure that they never encounter people or situations which they would otherwise have to master or submit to. In persons who regard home as safe and parents as protectors the phobic defence leads to an unwillingness to move away from home or to abandon familiar roles in favour of new ones – or even to explore new avenues of thought. As a result the person who uses phobic defences tends to lead a restricted life and to maintain the one role that is both safe and familiar, that of being a protected child who never strays far from home and parents. Since, however, there are forces in human nature which impel one away from the parental home and to abandon the role of child, the phobic has to repress his potential maturity and has to defend himself particularly against situations which might tempt him to abandon his position of safety. As a result he hates school and will avoid parties, dances, crowds and travel, not only because they lead him into unfamiliar territory but also because they offer encouragement to the active, enterprising, adult parts of himself that he is trying to disown.

However, in persons who regard home as stifling and parents as oppressors, the phobic defence goes into reverse and what I have just described is characteristic only of the potential agoraphobic, the person who is made anxious by open spaces. In the claustrophobic defence it is home and the familiar which arouses anxiety and the flight is away from the enclosed, safety and security only being experienced in the open. 'Don't fence me in' is the motto of the claustrophobic, who not only dreads being physically enclosed but also all social roles which pin him down and from which there appears to be no means of escape. As a result he will avoid marriage and office jobs with a fixed routine.

A more extreme example of flight is provided by the psychosis schizophrenia, in which the whole external world may be regarded as frightening and the patient becomes mute and inaccessible, withdrawing from external reality and living entirely in an inner world of fantasy which he has conjured up in compensation. Here again the flight is, in part at least, from an aspect of the self, the frightening external world being a projection of impulses that the schizophrenic has been unable to master within himself. Many schizophrenics believe that they are being persecuted by a machine which bombards them incessantly with malignant rays and compels them to experience sensations and thoughts which are not their own; according to a classic paper by Viktor Tausk this influencing machine is in fact the patient's own body from which he has become alienated so that he no longer recognizes its sensations as his own. Since the schizophrenic, unlike the phobic, regards the whole external world as frightening, schizoid flight is not a matter of avoiding particular situations which arouse anxiety and of finding other situations which provide security but rather of trying to escape completely from the physical world, and from the people in it. Since this is impossible, the schizophrenic has no choice but to deny that the physical world and the real people in it have any meaning for him and to live in an imaginary world of his own construction. Although schizophrenia is a psychosis, and therefore outside the scope of this book, the flight from reality into a private world of fantasy also occurs in the so-called schizoid character, whose contacts with others are reduced to the minimum necessary to provide him with the security within which to pursue his day-dreams without intrusion.

Flight implies not only movement away from danger but also movement towards safety, and flight towards safety occurs in both the phobic and schizoid defences. The phobic who feels anxious in open spaces feels safe when enclosed and at home, and one of the symptoms of phobia is in fact the phobic's belief in the protective power of his home or of some particular person, usually either his mother or spouse. This belief is just as irrational as the belief in the danger of the phobic situation, and the persons on whom phobics depend are in no way chosen for their actual strength and reliability or even for their devotion to the patient. As I mentioned in the introduction, a young woman who was unable to leave her home unless accompanied by her fiancé was involved with him in a car accident. Although neither of them was physically injured, he panicked and it was she who dealt with the situation, phoning for the police and giving first aid to the passengers in the other car. This experience did not, however, cure her of her phobia; nor did it cure her of her belief in her fiancé's capacity to protect her. The capacity of the phobic situation to provoke anxiety depends on its having acquired a symbolic meaning by projection, and that of the protecting situation or person to provide a feeling of security does so equally. The phobic defence is, in a sense, the opposite of the obsessional; instead of regarding himself as being in control of everything, the phobic regards himself as being at the mercy of fate, in perpetual danger from malevolent forces external to himself and owing his safety to the protection of benevolent Powers greater than himself. And instead of defending himself against anxiety by internalizing the environment, a procedure which reduces anxiety at the cost of increasing liability to guilt, the phobic defends himself against anxiety by negating himself, a procedure which reduces anxiety at the cost of maintaining the infantile sense of helplessness. The phobic defence can, indeed, be called the most naïve of the defences, since it reproduces one of the most elementary biological responses, the flight back to mother when danger threatens, and phobic illnesses can be regarded as manifestations of the conflict between the wish to grow up and leave mother and the wish to remain protected by her. In agoraphobics the wish to grow up is denied and projected, so that situations which would otherwise provide opportunities for learning self-reliance are experienced as frightening, while in claustrophobics the wish to remain protected is denied and projected, so that situations which would otherwise be enjoyed for their intimacy, cosiness and security are experienced as stifling.

The schizoid defence can be regarded as intermediate between the obsessional and the phobic. Like the phobic, but unlike the obsessional, the schizoid regards the outside world as frightening and beyond his control and he therefore tends to withdraw from it; but he fails to counterbalance this fear by developing any belief in the existence of benevolent agencies external to himself. He therefore finds the external world totally frightening and the only safety he knows is in his own imagination. As a result he becomes suspicious of all other human beings and instead of idealizing some actual person and instating him or her as a protecting mother-figure, he idealizes himself, imagining himself to be such an omnipotent figure that the need for protection does not arise. In extreme cases this leads to delusions of grandeur, in which the patient asserts that he is some important though fictitious personage. Freud once wrote a paper in which he analysed the delusional beliefs of a man who claimed to be Margrave of Tuscany and Tasmania, and I once had under my care a man who had dubbed himself Emperor of Australia. This process of self-idealization resembles the obsessional defence in that it is dependent on internalization, and on treating thoughts and words as though they had the reality which properly belongs only to their external referents. However, the schizoid defence differs from the obsessional in that the schizoid person makes no attempt to force real people into preconceived roles; he restricts himself to establishing mastery over a territory which is entirely fictitious and self-created.

Although both the phobic and the schizoid defences are forms of flight from danger, the threats to personal integrity which initiate them seem to be of a different order. Whereas the phobias seem to arise in persons whose upbringing has been overshadowed by 'over protective' or 'over-possessive' parents, who arouse anxiety either by painting the outside world in alarming colours or by interpreting signs of dawning self-reliance as defiance of their own authority but who are nonetheless content to allow their children to be human and spontaneous so long as they remain childish, schizoid disorders seem to occur in persons whose parents have little if any regard for their children as persons; the literature on schizophrenia abounds in references to 'schizophrenogenic mothers (and occasionally fathers) who treat their children as automata or dolls, who exist solely to be controlled and manipulated by them. Such parents seem to have no conception of the fact that children can have thoughts, feelings and preferences of their own. As a result of this difference in the quality of their upbringing, the phobic is capable of human relationships so long as he is in the dependent position but becomes anxious in situations which might help him to learn self-reliance, while the schizoid distrusts human contact as such and suspects the motives of anyone who makes overtures to him. He reacts, indeed, as though there were a difference of species between himself and other members of the human race and as though they were predators and he were their prey.

SUBMISSION AND THE HYSTERICAL DEFENCE

Although it used to be believed that nature was 'red in tooth and claw' and that animals of the same species frequently fought one another for possession of territory or mates, the researches of the ethological school of animal psychology, which studies animals under natural conditions and not in captivity, have shown that actual fighting between members of the same species is a rarity. According to Tinbergen, trials of strength between animals in rivalry 'usually consist of threatening or bluff', in which the stronger animal adopts a threatening posture, baring its teeth, growling and increasing its apparent size by pricking its ears, bristling its hair and extending its tail, while the weaker one takes up a submissive position, reducing its apparent size by crouching, drooping its tail and flattening its ears and hair. 'The outcome is typically the withdrawal of the inferior, without injury to either side' (S. A. Barnett). Even if there is an actual fight 'the losing wolf' according to Lorenz 'in the wolf-fight asks for and receives mercy'.

Much the same thing happens in trials of strength between individual human beings. When we are being self-assertive, proud or authoritative and are trying to assert our will over others, we raise our voices, draw ourselves up to our full height and do everything we can to convey the impression that we are someone to be reckoned with, whereas when we are feeling diffident, ashamed or obsequious and wish to mitigate the wrath of someone more powerful than ourselves, we bow our heads, speak quietly or haltingly and actually or metaphorically kowtow. Although, owing to human self-consciousness, both postures may be feigned on occasions when we need to appear more self-assured or humble than we actually feel, this only increases the subtlety of the bluff that goes on in trials of strength and struggles for power between individuals, which only rarely lead to physical fights and even more rarely to fights to the death.

The self-assertive posture is a form of the attack or mastery response and cannot be regarded as neurotic, though feigned self-assertion may on occasion be. Nor is submission always neurotic; it may be the only possible response to an encounter in which we are the physical, psychological or social inferior and therefore have no choice but to retire 'with our tail between our legs'. Conflicts of will between human beings are, however, perhaps less likely to end with the total victory of one and the complete surrender of the other than in animals, owing to the fact that human aims are more complex and multifarious; as a result conflicts of will can be resolved by compromises in which both parties achieve some of their aims and neither loses face completely. Nor is it always obvious which of the two parties is the more dominant, since the physical, psychological and social factors which determine human 'pecking order' may be at variance with one another. If a shy and ailing schoolmaster has to assert his authority over a self–assured eighteen-year-old tough, it is by no means obvious with whom victory will lie or which will feel small at the end of the interview.

However, the long biological childhood of human beings, which is still further prolonged by the social conventions which allow parents to retain a measure of financial and legal control over their children for some years after they are physically mature, creates a situation in which conflicts of will inside the family – including the Oedipal rivalry between father and son and mother and daughter – may be resolved by the child habitually adopting a submissive attitude which persists into adult life, and which forms the basis of the hysterical defence. The tendency of children to adopt the submissive role must have been enhanced in the Victorian era, when many parents invoked God as the source of their authority and considered it their religious duty to break their children's will.

The submissive response to situations of rivalry and competition is responsible for neurotic passivity in men. In situations in which it would be appropriate to be assertive and forceful neurotically passive men habitually present themselves as feeble, ingratiating and ineffective. In such men the anxiety induced by competitive situations and by taking responsibility arises not only from the present trial of strength but also from two other sources; the childhood struggle for power with whichever parent dominated them, and fear lest the aggression, which was repressed when they adopted the submissive attitude, should return from repression. In the last resort such men are more frightened of their own aggression than they are of that of others.

The extreme form of neurotic passivity in men, which leads not only to social ineffectiveness but also to sexual impotence, seems to occur in men who originally adopted the submissive attitude as a response to an active, masculine, domineering mother and who therefore take up an habitually passive attitude towards women which is incompatible with heterosexual activity. Acceptance of the submissive role may also lead passive men to marry active, dominating women with whom they can reproduce the situation to which they became acclimatized as a child; such marriages are usually only a qualified success.

Passive men are often described as feminine or as latent homosexuals, but 'effeminate' is really the appropriate qualifier, since the stance they adopt and the helplessness they display is more like that of a neurotic woman than a healthy one and psychotherapy never turns them into manifest homosexuals. The submissive defence used by passive men would, I believe, be generally recognized as hysterical if it were not for the resistance to applying to men a word which derives from the Greek for womb.

In some ways, however, the hysterical or submissive defence is exemplified more clearly in men than in women, since in the latter the picture is confused by the traditional tendency to regard women as naturally passive and submissive, a man-made tradition which leads some women to affect in the presence of men a submissiveness which they do not in fact feel, and which has led some psychologists, including Freud himself, to explain feminine adaptability and responsiveness in terms of passivity and masochism. However, even if one rejects, as I would, the view that women are inherently submissive or hysterical, there remains nonetheless a class of women who regard themselves as fundamentally defeated and who consistently adopt a submissive attitude in their relations to both men and other women, and whose character is therefore analogous to that of the passive men whom I have already described. Such women allow themselves to be used as doormats or dolls by men and are incapable of asserting their own right to self-fulfilment – I have even known young women who allowed themselves to be sterilized solely because their husbands disliked children – or of competing with other women as women. They let themselves be put upon by possessive parents or selfish husbands and adopt a long-suffering attitude if their husbands are unfaithful or if their lovers treat them as a convenience. As in the case of passive men, neurotic submissiveness in women is not primarily due to contemporary anxiety about standing up to men or competing with other women; it is the result of a prior act of submission in childhood which has undermined their self-respect and which has compelled them to repress all self-assertive tendencies. As a result any adult situation which demands self-assertion evokes not only normal anxiety but also signal-anxiety in respect of their repressed hostility. If, as sometimes happens in psychotherapy, the worm turns, the erstwhile submissive woman will suddenly be transformed into a militant advocate of her own rights, to the great discomfiture of her previous exploiters.

Habitual adoption of the hysterical, submissive defence does not abolish aggression and self-assertion but sends it underground and in persons who use this defence extensively 'the return of the repressed' manifests itself in devious forms. Either the worm will turn intermittently, leading to short-lived and ineffective 'hysterical' attacks of rage, or the submissive role will itself be exploited in a way calculated to control others by making them feel guilty, or the conviction of being a defeated person will be used to justify underhand methods of manipulating others. It is this last, the use of guile in situations in which persons with self-respect are direct and open, which is responsible for the general dislike and disapproval of hysterical behaviour and which led the French neurologist Lhermitte to remark that 'hysteria is the mother of deceit and trickery'. The best documented form of hysterical guile is the development of hysterical conversion-symptoms which simulate physical illness. Given the conscious assumption that he is weak and worthless and is an object of no interest or importance to others, the hysteric can only gain attention and get his own way by exaggerating his weakness and using the idea of illness as a weapon with which to control others or to evoke mercy. In a situation in which a self-assured person would openly refuse to do something and would give his grounds for doing so, the hysterical person will become ill and therefore unable to do it. Unfortunately for the hysterical defence, the forms of disability which can be induced psychologically are often easily distinguished from organic illness and the defence may miscarry. He or she will then be accused of malingering or imagining an illness, which is an unfair half-truth unless it is accompanied by some explanation of why it has been found necessary to adopt such a desperate and unself-respecting solution of problems. The accusation is also usually unfair in another sense; it assumes that the hysteric has insight into his own motives and has simulated the illness with full deliberation. This is only rarely the case.

In the previous paragraph I have described how the technique of exploiting the submissive attitude may be used by hysterics to control those whom they imagine to be more dominant than themselves and whom they therefore feel unable to master openly or to negotiate with as equals; I have attributed this preference for using the submissive response to a feeling of having been defeated in childhood struggles for power, love and attention. This sense of being defeated persons confronts them with two psychological problems, one practical and the other emotional; the former being how to deal with a world in which everyone is conceived to have more powers and rights than themselves, and the latter being how to keep repressed the hostility and resentment engendered by having been pushed into the submissive role. Hysterical symptoms help with both problems since they simultaneously provide a means by which helplessness can itself be converted into an instrument of power and a technique for putting out of action all the functions which an openly aggressive person might use to give vent to his hostility. A woman during analytical treatment experienced the end of every session and the week-end break as slights which demonstrated her powerlessness to influence her analyst. At the end of one Friday session she developed a paralysis of both legs. This not only enabled her to remain longer on the couch than was her due and to convey the impression that she was really too ill to be left unattended for a whole week-end but also prevented her from kicking her analyst or getting up and hitting him. The same patient lost her voice – developed an hysterical aphonia – at the end of another Friday session. Here again the analyst was meant to feel that he must be a heartless creature to allow her to go away so seriously disturbed and disabled; at the same time it prevented her abusing him. It was also a form of sulking – if he wouldn't speak to her, she wouldn't – couldn't – speak to anyone.

The sexual disabilities from which hysterical women suffer fulfil a similar dual function, though analysts do not, of course, observe this directly. Convinced that they are unworthy of love, and that men are more powerful and important than women, their frigidity enables them to withhold what they believe never was and never will be given to them – and to wield power over men by so withholding themselves – while at the same time it prevents them from getting into a spontaneously impassioned state in which they might be tempted to give free rein to hostile as well as loving feelings. It also symbolizes their conviction that they have been totally defeated in the Oedipal struggle with their mothers and that they are therefore incapable of possessing a husband themselves. Although this conviction of having been defeated by their mother derives from childhood, it is increased by the fact that girls reach womanhood during their mothers' middle age; they may therefore, if already predisposed, avoid their mothers' envy and jealousy by an act of sexual renunciation. In contemporary society, which allows women to adopt careers, this acceptance of defeat by the mother is often masked by an assumed preference for the masculine role. Unfortunately the English language lacks a word which bears the same relation to 'masculine' as 'effeminate' does to 'feminine'; and yet many confirmed professional women betray the falsity of their masculinity by a peculiar stridency and push from which masculine men are free.

In this account of the hysterical defence, I have been guided more by my own experience than by the literature, which can be searched in vain for a satisfactory or coherent account of the sort of childhood which predisposes to hysteria. According to Freud's original formulations hysterical women suffer from penis-envy, while the later literature emphasizes the importance of domination by, and fear of, a pre-Oedipal 'phallic' mother. Both these formulations imply that the future hysteric has felt herself overshadowed by persons more forceful than herself and they can, it seems to me, both be subsumed under the common head of a sense of having been defeated and forced into a submissive role, which leaves the victim feeling consciously helpless and inadequate and unconsciously envious and resentful. Certainly, all the hysterics whom I have treated, both the men and the women, have gone through childhoods which have left them deeply convinced of their own insignificance and that their parents have been primarily preoccupied with their own lives and not with those of their children. They have been handed over to nurses at an early age, if not at birth, have been sent young to boarding schools and convents and often left there during the holidays as well, or have been lent to grandmothers or maiden aunts who have felt lonely without a child in the house, and have been returned home when their presence was no longer convenient. If girls, they have been left in no doubt that their brothers are of more importance than themselves and that the real world is a male one into which they have no entry. Unlike the phobics who have been over-protected, and the schizoids who have been brought up according to rigid parental preconceptions which entirely ignored their own sensibilities, the hysterics have been pushed around and neglected – not materially, since they have often been spoilt in the sense of being bribed by expensive presents and treats to accept their neglect, but emotionally in terms of lack of personal consideration and understanding.

In the three preceding sections I have tried to correlate the obsessional, phobic, schizoid and hysterical defences with the three biological responses, attack, flight and submission. In doing so I have been compelled for expository reasons to make two simplifications which I must now correct. Firstly, I have described the defences as though they occur in isolation from one another, as though the use of one defence precluded the use of the others. This is not so. Although it is possible to encounter individuals who appear at first sight to be out-and-out obsessionals or hysterics, closer acquaintance always reveals the presence of the other defences. Psycho-analysts, who spend their lives in close contact with a few patients whom they get to know intimately, often become very sceptical about the value of diagnostic labels, but psychiatrists, who see many patients and who have to make diagnoses, prognoses and recommendations for treatment on the basis of perhaps only a single interview, usually have very little difficulty in ascertaining which of the four defences is predominant.

Secondly, I have described each defence as though it were based exclusively on the use of only one biological response.

This again is not correct; the obsessional defence consists not only of mastery of the self and others but also of submission towards the internalized authority which commands them to master emotion; the phobic defence is not only flight from the outside world but also submission to the internalized injunction 'Thou shalt not grow up'; the schizoid defence allows mastery to flourish, and indeed luxuriate, in fantasy; and the hysterical defence includes an underground attack on authority and an attempt to escape from it. The defences I have described are, therefore, not to be thought of as simply the psychological equivalents of individual, isolated biological responses but as complex strategies, in which one particular response, mastery, flight or submission, occupies a nodal position. Generals commanding armies do not conduct campaigns only by attacking, or retreating, or surrendering positions, while the significance of one tactical move is only comprehensible in terms of the overall strategy; retreat may be an example of '*reculer pour mieux sauter*', an attack on one sector may be to cover a retreat on another, and surrender of one position may be a means of preserving another. Just as some generals become expert at one strategy – think of Napoleon, Fabius Cunctator and Stonewall Jackson – so the neurotic need to defend personal integrity against imagined (though often once real) threats leads to the development of characteristic modes of defence.

Chapter 6

The Neuroses

The defences which I described in the previous chapter are not in themselves neurotic. Just as everyone is at times anxious, so everyone at times uses defences, and the use of one or other of these defences can only be regarded as neurotic if it becomes habitual and is resorted to under circumstances in which there is no need to use defences at all, or in which it would be more appropriate or efficient to use some other defence. The person who always tries to master situations obsessionally, who always avoids dangers, or who always submits to others, is behaving neurotically since his behaviour has ceased to be spontaneous and has become subject to restrictions which limit his capacity for enjoyment and self-development. Such persons are said to be suffering from a character-neurosis, the 'symptom' of which is the subjective sense of being held up by compulsive traits of character. They are not, however, ill in the ordinary sense of the term, since what they complain of is not some symptom which intrudes on their otherwise normal personality but an aspect of the personality itself which both they and those around them may regard as an essential part of themselves. It is indeed possible for persons with character-neuroses to reject completely the idea that there is anything the matter with them and to regard as normal, or perhaps even meritorious, precisely those traits of character which would lead a psychiatrist to diagnose them as neurotic. This happens most frequently in the case of persons who use obsessional and schizoid defences; the phobic and hysterical defences do not provide their users with any sense of their own superiority.

Neurosis in its true sense only occurs when defences begin to fail. When this happens, wishes, fears, memories and fantasies, which the defences have previously kept unconscious, begin to re-emerge and the individual experiences conscious anxiety and develops symptoms. Since defences purchase stability at the cost of restrictions of personality and behaviour, there is something paradoxical about the onset of a neurosis. On the one hand it is a matter of falling ill, becoming anxious and developing symptoms, but on the other it is a matter of a previously rigid personality going into flux again and it therefore offers an opportunity for widening of the personality and re-integration at a higher level. Whether such a happy outcome actually occurs depends, of course, on a variety of circumstances, one of which is whether the incipient neurotic has the good fortune to encounter a psychotherapist before he has become set in a neurotic pattern of life. Another is the attitude of his family. Many a neurotic has had things made worse for him by relatives who insist that he pull himself together – advice which is usually useless, since it is asking him to return to the *status quo ante* which he has already found untenable – or who themselves become so anxious that his neurotic anxiety is compounded by his discovery that those whose support he needs need his.

Although it is, regrettably, rather unusual for persons who are developing a neurosis to receive psychotherapeutic help before their neurosis has become chronic, by no means everyone who develops neurotic symptoms goes on to become permanently ill. Sometimes the symptoms are part and parcel of some spontaneous revolution of personality, as may happen in adolescence and the early twenties, and cease when the crisis is over. Sometimes the environment may prove more flexible and amenable than the 'patient' believed it to be and he may be able to reorganize his life in a way that solves the conflict which precipitated his neurosis. The young man whose nightmare of falling into machinery I described in Chapter 2, did not develop a chronic neurosis. His parents seemed to be able to tolerate with equanimity his going through a phase of being very aggressive towards them, and when he summoned up enough courage to choose a career for himself, they put no obstacles in his way.

However, despite the existence of short-lived neuroses which disappear when the crisis, internal or external, which precipitated it is over, some do become chronic, and for the rest of this chapter I shall be discussing those neurotic states which last long enough and are sufficiently disabling for their victims to seek medical help. Such neuroses are the ones which constitute the problem of neurosis as it confronts the medical profession and which is responsible for an enormous amount of human unhappiness and wastage of potential. It is estimated that in a practice of 2,500 patients, 175 adults will consult their general practitioner each year on account of a neurotic illness. This figure works out at about ten per cent of the adult population, and it is more likely to be an under-estimate than an exaggeration. Neurosis is not a notifiable disease: many persons with neuroses never consult a doctor about it, some are compatible with full working efficiency despite creating havoc in the victim's personal life, and others manifest themselves as inhibitions which the sufferer accepts as an inevitable restriction on his life – and it is probably still more common for neuroses to be misdiagnosed as physical illnesses than for physical illness to be treated as a neurosis.

THE DIAGNOSIS OF NEUROSIS

Once a person has developed a neurosis and has sought medical treatment for it, he becomes subject to the medical procedure of diagnosis. The purpose of diagnosis is, of course, to discover which medically-recognized disease the patient is suffering from. Although this can sometimes be done by the simple process of recognizing that the patient is exhibiting the signs and symptoms of a familiar clinical entity, the full diagnostic procedure consists in also excluding all other possibilities. This latter aspect of diagnosis is of considerable importance in the neuroses, since neurotic symptoms may simulate those of physical illness and both doctors and the general public account it a greater mistake to misdiagnose a physical illness as a neurosis than to make the opposite mistake. This preference is partly due to the feeling that it is more respectable to have a physical illness than a neurosis, but it also has better reasons. The neurotic symptoms which simulate physical symptoms do not as a rule threaten life, while physical conditions which simulate neurosis sometimes do – an example is cerebral tumour of which the only symptom at first may be headache, a common neurotic symptom – and the treatment of physical illnesses is in general better understood and standardized than that of the neuroses.

Neuroses do not, however, only require differentiation from physical illness; they also have to be distinguished from two other psychiatric conditions; the psychoses and the behaviour-disorders, which differ from the neuroses not only in respect of their symptoms but also in their treatment and prognosis. In the next three sections I shall, therefore, give a brief account of how the neuroses differ from physical illness, psychosis and the behaviour-disorders.

NEUROSIS AND PHYSICAL ILLNESS

Since the symptoms of a neurosis may include complaints of physical distress, the first stage in the diagnosis of a neurosis is to ascertain that there are no signs of organic illness. If the patient is anxious, diseases like thyrotoxicosis (Graves's Disease), which disturb the physiological mechanisms underlying vigilance and thereby induce anxiety, have to be excluded, while the physical effects of psychogenic anxiety, such as palpitations and diarrhoea, have to be shown not to be due to heart or intestinal disease. If the patient complains of a paralysed limb, or blindness, or of a lump in the throat, the physical complaint has to be shown *not* to correspond to how the body actually works but to reflect the patient's preconceptions as to how his body works. As I mentioned earlier, the exclusion of physical illness depends on the fact that physiological and anatomical knowledge is sufficiently well-established for the examining physician to be able to rely on what he himself observes rather than on what the patient tells him, and to be able to demonstrate that hysterical physical complaints make anatomical and physiological nonsense.

Since, however, medical knowledge and methods of examination are not perfect, the proof that any physical complaint is in fact of psychological origin cannot be based solely on the negative evidence that all known physical illnesses have been excluded. It requires in addition positive evidence that the symptom fulfils a psychological function. In principle, this can be done in two different ways: by ascertaining the circumstances in which it first occurred and which exacerbate it, and by observing the patient's attitude towards his symptom. Symptoms which only occur on the last days of the holidays or only in the morning just before leaving for school or work, or only when the in-laws come to stay, are likely to be neurotic. If a patient appears curiously undistressed by a symptom which on the face of it should be disastrously incapacitating, or if he describes his symptoms with relish, the likelihood is that the patient is gaining some advantage from his symptoms. Although these methods sound very subjective, experienced physicians often become very astute in detecting hysterical and neurotic demeanours and are more likely to be caught out by the occasions on which a neurotic develops a physical illness than they are to misdiagnose a neurosis as a physical illness. Hysterical personalities who develop physical illness do, however, sometimes have difficulty in persuading anyone to take it seriously. In such cases the principle of Cry Wolf is in operation.

NEUROSIS AND PSYCHOSIS

The next stage in the diagnosis of a neurosis is exclusion of the possibility of psychosis. The psychoses are the major psychiatric illnesses and they differ from the neuroses in that the patient's reflective capacity is grossly disturbed, so that he loses insight into the fact that he is ill and behaves as though his abnormal thoughts and moods were valid. Both normal and neurotic people know what kinds of thoughts they have and can distinguish clearly between realistic thought and day-dreaming, between serious activity and play, between thinking literally and metaphorically, and between feeling guilty and being guilty. In other words, they appreciate the logical status of every thought and action and even though they may have day-dreams that they are someone else, they know that it is only a day-dream; or if they feel compelled to perform some obsessional ritual and *feel* that it is necessary if they are to ward off a sense of impending danger, they *know* that the action is pointless and superstitious; or if they are depressed and feel as though they had committed some terrible crime, they know that this is a mood they are in and that it is not valid. In psychosis, however, this ability to evaluate thoughts, actions and moods in the light of common sense and to assess their significance and place in the totality of their being is lost. As a result night-mares and day-dreams become delusions, and moods of depression and elation are acted on. This loss of insight has, of course, dangerous consequences for both the patient and society, since he may take action which is based on delu-sional premises. If he has delusions of grandeur, he may act as though he is someone else or take the law into his own hands, even to the point of murder; if he is elated he may spend money which he hasn't got; if depressed, he may rid the world of the evil being he believes himself to be by committing suicide; if he believes his food is being poisoned, he may die of starvation. As a result, the distinction between psychosis and neurosis is virtually the same as that between insanity and sanity, and to diagnose someone as neurotic is to affirm that he is capable of managing his own affairs and of living outside an institution.

Controversy exists as to whether the psychoses and neuroses differ in kind or merely in severity. Although it is generally agreed that the neuroses are psychological disturb-ances which can occur in persons who are physically healthy, opinion is divided as to whether the so-called functional psychoses – schizophrenia and manic-depressive psychosis – are due to some as yet undiscovered biochemical, metabolic or genetic disorder or whether they are psychological disturbances capable of the same kind of explanation as the neuroses. Psychiatrists who believe the former can cite an extensive literature attributing psychosis to specific physical causes, although none of the suggested causes has ever received the general and immediate acceptance which is usual in medicine when the cause of some previously mysterious disease is finally elucidated. Psychiatrists who believe the latter attribute the psychoses either to traumata and emo-tional deprivation of greater severity occurring earlier in life than those responsible for the neuroses, or to the use of different defensive techniques. Indeed, according to one theory, that originally propounded in 1956 by Gregory

Bateson *et al.* in their paper 'Towards a Theory of Schizophrenia',* the loss of insight characteristic of psychosis is not basically an incapacity or defect at all but itself a defensive manoeuvre by which the psychotic patient has protected himself from contradictory and impossible emotional demands made on him in childhood by putting out of action his capacity to distinguish between different orders and nuances of thought or feeling. According to this view, the psychotic preserves his integrity by an apparent sacrifice of it, his identity by becoming a nonentity, and his sensibility by becoming impervious. In this country, Laing, Esterson and Cooper are the most enthusiastic advocates of this view of psychosis.

However, whatever view is taken of the cause and nature of psychosis, the important practical difference between psychosis and neurosis is that the former is a disorder of the total personality, whereas the latter is a partial, circumscribed disorder occurring in persons whose sanity is not in doubt and whose cooperation in treatment can be relied upon. As a result the neuroses are accessible to psychotherapy, since the neurotic is capable of forming a 'therapeutic alliance' with

* This paper contains the first statement of the 'double-bind' hypothesis of the origin of schizophrenia. This hypothesis, the germ of which first occurred to Bateson while making an anthropological study of the impact of Western cultural values on primitive tribes in New Guinea, states that the effect of subjecting an individual – or a culture – to contradictory pressures may be to compel him to abandon the capacity to distinguish between different categories of thought, as a result of which he may become confused and mystified and lose faith in the accuracy of his perceptions. He may, for instance, cease to be able to distinguish between his own perception of what another is feeling and what that other says he is feeling, or between what he himself is feeling and what others say he is feeling. This confusion will only become persistent and pathogenic if (*a*) the experience of being in a 'double-bind' is frequent (*b*) the 'binder' has superior status in the eyes of the 'victim' and (*c*) the 'victim' has no avenue of escape. When applied to the causation of schizophrenia, the theory asserts that one parent of the future schizophrenic, usually the mother, habitually enforces a false perception of their relationship on him, and that he, by reason of his immaturity and dependence, is unable to escape from her influence or to sustain his own vision of the true state of affairs.

his therapist, the sane and healthy part of his personality being capable of reflecting upon the nature and origin of his symptoms and of participating in their elucidation.

NEUROSIS AND THE BEHAVIOUR-DISORDERS

The third stage in the diagnosis of a neurosis is its differentiation from the so-called behaviour-or personality-disorders. Whereas the neuroses are characterized by anxiety, inhibition and symptoms of a private and restrictive nature, the behaviour–disorders are characterized by behaviour which causes the individual no anxiety or sense of inner conflict but which marks him out as deviant, abnormal or eccentric, and which may bring him into conflict with society. Sexual perverts, drug addicts, alcoholics, psychopaths, delinquents and some eccentrics are considered by psychiatrists to be suffering from behaviour-disorders, though they do not usually regard themselves as ill. Nor has society as a whole accepted the view that they should be regarded as ill.

The concept of behaviour-disorder is indeed a very peculiar one. Illnesses are in general phenomena which cause suffering primarily to the subject afflicted himself. Although the relatives of a patient with anaemia or pneumonia may be distressed and inconvenienced by his illness, there can be no doubt that the main sufferer is the patient himself. The same is true of both the psychoses and the neuroses. If a person is deluded, depressed, impotent or plagued by obsessions, the main sufferer is undoubtedly the patient himself, and there is also no doubt that he would rather be relieved of his symptoms than retain them. Nor would anyone seriously argue that being deluded, depressed, impotent or obsessed are states of mind that should be judged morally.

In the case of homosexuals, delinquents, drug addicts and drunkards, however, none of the assumptions implicit in the concept of illness can be taken for granted. It is by no means obvious that it is homosexuals and drunkards who *suffer* from homosexuality and alcoholism, nor is it obvious that they want to be 'cured' of their 'illness'. And society is by no means unanimous in regarding the behaviour-disorders as objects for therapeutic concern; they are also disapproved of and regarded as in need of punishment, not treatment. Indeed, the behaviour-disorders appear at first sight to differ from physical illness, psychosis and neurosis in being primarily social and not medical problems, in causing distress to others rather than to themselves, and in being conditions which provoke social disapproval rather than therapeutic concern.

One reason for this disapproval is that the 'symptoms' of behaviour-disorders are in themselves pleasurable. Homosexuals claim to enjoy homosexual acts, and drunkards to enjoy drinking, while delinquents either enjoy or gain material advantage from their delinquent acts, even though the initial pleasure or advantage may be followed by unpleasant consequences. Homosexuals do not in general enjoy the prospect of a childless middle and old age, drunkards do not enjoy either their hangovers or their cirrhosis of the liver; nor do delinquents enjoy imprisonment. The tendency to disapprove of persons with behaviour-disorders derives, then, from the fact that their actions are not only anti-social but also, apparently at least, voluntary and pleasurable. The idea of other people actually getting pleasure from behaviour which one finds distasteful or disgusting (as in the case of the perversions) or which one has been too well brought up to consider engaging in oneself (as in the case of delinquency) is liable to provoke envy, and hence moral disapproval, more readily than compassion. A compassionate and therapeutic reaction is only likely to be evoked when one considers the long-term effects of the behaviour-disorders.

There are, however, other reasons for regarding the behaviour-disorders as illnesses, in addition to the fact that their late effects may evoke sympathy. The first is that closer clinical observation reveals that persons suffering from behaviour-disorders are not altogether unlike persons suffering from other psychiatric disorders. Some of the behaviour-disorders can, indeed, be fitted into the theoretical framework which I have used to elucidate the neuroses. Male homosexuality, for instance, can be regarded as a mixture of flight from women and submission towards men, the need for both defensive manoeuvres being referable to the emotional climate of their childhood. Alcoholism and drug-addiction can both be regarded as ways of reducing neurotic anxiety and depression pharmacologically and as forms of unconscious self-medication which caricature the tendency of organically-minded physicians to treat anxiety with sedatives and depression with stimulants.

The behaviour-disorders seem, in fact, to resemble the neuroses in being responses to, and defences against, neurotic anxiety, but differ from them in that the anxiety tends to be relieved by precipitate action and not mastered by inhibition, and that problems of maladaptation tend to be dealt with by attempts to alter the outside world or the state of the body rather than by psychological alteration of the self. The behaviour-disorders are examples of alloplastic maladaptation and the neuroses examples of autoplastic maladaptation, to use a distinction first made by Franz Alexander. The resemblance between the behaviour-disorders and the neuroses is reflected in the fact that popular usage has come to describe both as 'neurotic'.

Another reason for regarding the behaviour-disorders as illnesses is that they tend to be self-destructive. Alcoholics and drug addicts actively harm their bodies and reduce their expectation of life while delinquents and psychopaths dissipate their aggressive energies in isolated destructive acts which inevitably rebound on themselves.

Although the extreme liberal position is that people have a right to destroy themselves or to waste their talents, if they so wish, society as a whole thinks differently. Until recently suicide, the self-destructive act *par excellence*, was a criminal offence, the historical explanation for this being that suicide is regarded by the Church as an offence against Natural Law and therefore a sin. In an increasingly secular society, the enforcement of Canon Law by the civil courts was an anachronism, but the fact that suicide is no longer a crime does not mean that it has become an act to which society is indifferent; suicide remains a phenomenon with which society is concerned, quite regardless as to whether its individual members view it as a sin, a crime or a symptom, or whether it is the responsibility of the Church, the law or the medical profession. Similarly, the behaviour-disorders concern society, and in the absence of any effective means by which either the clergy or the law can help them, their treatment goes by default to the psychiatrists, the social fiction that they are illnesses providing the theoretical justification for an approach towards them which is neither exhortatory nor retributive but therapeutic. However, since the behaviour-disorders give rise to social problems in a way that neuroses in the strict sense never do, their treatment is unlikely ever to become the sole preserve of the medical profession, and we are unlikely ever to reach the situation envisaged in Samuel Butler's *Erewhon*, in which all criminality was considered an illness.

NEUROSIS, UNHAPPINESS AND ANOMIE

There are two other conditions with which neurosis may be confused, though neither of them is medical or psychiatric. One is unhappiness. Although neurotics suffer, and must therefore be regarded as to some extent unhappy, the reverse proposition that all unhappiness is neurotic does not follow. In this respect unhappiness resembles anxiety and depression. It may be due to repressed unconscious factors but it may also be the appropriate and inevitable response to adverse present circumstances. The idea that the ideally healthy person would always be happy is, indeed, even more absurd than the idea that such a person would never be anxious; it ignores such obvious social factors as poverty and war and the fact that mental health offers no immunity to disappointments in love or at work. It also assumes that the happiness of a single individual is independent of those around him. In fact, except for those rare narcissistic characters who, like the Miller of Dee, can sing cheerfully 'I care for nobody and nobody cares for me', happiness seems to depend as much on the well-being of those one cares for and on the success of causes and projects with which one identifies oneself as it does on one's own personal stability and health. Freud once remarked that the aim of psycho-analysis was to replace neurotic suffering by ordinary unhappiness. The half-truth concealed in this pessimistic remark is, I think, that the suffering of the neurotic is a private, self-orientated experience which protects him from those kinds of pain and disappointment which are dependent on active participation in life.

The other is the sense of uprootedness known to sociologists as *'anomie'*. This term was originally used by the French sociologist Emile Durkheim to describe the state of being released from the restraints of traditional, conventional social roles and values which he believed was responsible for one class of suicides, and is now used by, among others, Riesman in *The Lonely Crowd* to describe the state of anyone who is 'maladjusted' and at odds with the conventions. In this wider sense *anomie* is displayed not only by those whose lives have been confused and disrupted by rapid social change but also by those who actively reject conventional ways of living. Psychiatrists who are themselves conformists may be tempted to regard all non-conformists as neurotic, but if they do, they are really making a value-judgement and equating mental health with conformity to the way of life of which they themselves happen to approve – an attitude which, if taken to its logical conclusion, would transform psychiatrists from therapists into custodians of the Establishment. Anomic persons may be lonely and have a sense of not belonging anywhere, but they are not necessarily neurotic, since their *anomie* may be socially, not psychologically, determined. Refugees and immigrants who have not had time or opportunity to establish themselves, and the aged and infirm who lack responsible relatives and are victims of inadequacies in the social services, may become isolated and unhappy and even commit suicide, but they do not necessarily develop symptoms; and if they do, these are likely to be appeals for help and not manifestations of unconscious conflict. Neurosis can, however, lead to *anomie*, particularly in neurotics who use schizoid and phobic defences, since the withdrawal from others entailed by these defences may eventually lead to their actual social isolation. A phobic person who never leaves his home, or a schizoid person who rejects out of suspicion all friendly overtures made to him, will in the course of time lose touch with friends and relatives and become as isolated as those whose social difficulties are primarily environmental.

THE CLASSIFICATION OF NEUROSES

Once it has been established that a patient's anxiety and other symptoms are neurotic, it remains to be decided which of the various types of neurosis he is suffering from. The term 'neurosis' by itself is an insufficient diagnosis, since it merely indicates that the patient is ill, and not simply lonely or unhappy, and that the physicians who have examined him are reasonably certain that he is not physically ill and is not suffering from one or other of the major psychiatric disorders.

The next step is to decide which particular neurosis the patient has. Unfortunately this is not as straightforward or standardized a procedure as it might be, owing to the fact that psychiatry remains a branch of medicine afflicted by theoretical differences of opinion, which are reflected not only in different theories of causation but also in differing diagnostic habits. As a result, patients who have the misfortune to be passed rapidly from one psychiatrist or psychiatric institution to another, may collect a series of incompatible diagnoses which reflect the interests of the examining psychiatrists more accurately than their own clinical state. I once saw a young man who had been an in-patient in three mental institutions during the previous six months and had been diagnosed 'psychopathic personality' in the first, schizophrenic in the second, and 'neurotic reactive depression with obsessive features' in the third. The first institution specialized in psychopathic personalities, the second practised what was then the progressive policy of diagnosing and treating schizophrenia before its symptoms had become manifest – cynics would say when they were absent – while the third specialized in psychotherapy.

A further difficulty arises from the fact that neurotic symptoms are highly personal and are not of a kind that a patient can enumerate to a perfect stranger in a calm and detached manner. As a result, psychiatrists with differing personalities and interviewing techniques may elicit different aspects of a patient's history, problems and symptomatology, and may thus arrive at different diagnoses.

It is, therefore, not surprising that many psychiatrists and psychotherapists are sceptical of the value of diagnostic labels, particularly short ones like hysteria or obsessional neurosis, and prefer what are known as 'dynamic formulations'. 'Neurotic reactive depression with obsessive tendencies' is a typical dynamic formulation; it informs other psychiatrists that the patient is depressed, that it is not a psychotic depression, that it is believed to have been either precipitated or caused by some recent event, and that the patient is thought to use predominantly obsessional defences.

However, despite these difficulties, sub-division of the general category 'neurosis' into a number of specific neuroses remains necessary, if only because psychiatrists have to write something on the top of their case-sheets and because some sort of classification is necessary for statistical purposes. It is a procedure which also has heuristic value, inasmuch as it enables the complex phenomenology of the neuroses to be formulated in terms of a number of ideal and easily recognized 'clinical pictures' which actual living patients can be said to resemble more or less closely.

In view of what I have said in previous chapters, it might be expected that the general category 'neurosis' would be divided into four specific neuroses: the obsessional, schizoid, phobic and hysterical. However, this is not so. Although I personally believe that such a classification would be both theoretically possible and practically useful, it does not in fact correspond to the diagnostic habits of either psychiatrists in general or of any particular school. Nor does it correspond to the International Classification of Diseases or the American Psychiatric Association's Standard Nomenclature. Although obsessional neurosis, phobia (or phobic illness) and hysteria are diagnostic terms in general use, schizoid neurosis is a term never used, and two other diagnoses, anxiety-neurosis (or anxiety-state) and neurotic depression often are.

The lack of any category 'schizoid neurosis' means, of course, that patients whom I would be inclined to diagnose as schizoid neurotics, must in practice receive some other diagnosis. In the psycho-analytical literature the term 'schizoid-obsessional' is often encountered, and both hysterical and phobic illnesses are often interpreted as having an underlying schizoid pathology. The reason for this scattering of patients who use schizoid defences among the other diagnostic groupings is historical. The term 'schizoid' was originally introduced by Eugen Bleuler to describe the personality (and not the symptoms) of patients who resemble schizophrenics in that they are aloof, withdrawn and keep their intellectual and emotional lives in separate departments, but who are not deluded or hallucinating and are clearly not insane. Since it is the personalities of such patients, rather than their symptoms, which impress the psychiatrist, they tend to be called schizoid personalities or characters and not schizoid neurotics. Of recent years, however, largely owing to the work of Fairbairn and Melanie Klein, the peculiar splitting or dissociation of the personality which these patients display – and to which the word 'schizoid' specifically refers – has increasingly come to be regarded as a defensive manoeuvre which can also be observed in patients who would not be diagnosed as schizoid personalities. As a result schizoid defences can be observed in persons who are undoubtedly neurotic and who do not convey the impression of being potential schizophrenics, and patients who use such defences extensively might well be called schizoid neurotics. Such patients do in fact complain of symptoms, such as shyness, blushing, doubts about their identity and a sense of futility, all of which seem to derive from their acute perception of the discrepancy between their ideal self-image and the humdrum impression they actually make on the world.

ANXIETY-NEUROSIS

The term 'anxiety-neurosis' is used to describe all patients whose symptom is predominantly anxiety itself, although most psychiatrists regard the phobias, in which the anxiety is provoked by specific situations, as either a separate clinical entity or as a form of obsessional neurosis.

Patients who are said to be suffering from an anxiety-neurosis complain of being anxious, tense, irritable, worried, 'on edge', 'strung-up', etc., and they are, or claim to be, persistently anxious. Their anxiety is 'free-floating', in the sense that it may, unless they are phobic, be provoked by any and every circumstance and forms a background to everything they do.

It is, of course, impossible to give a single, specific

explanation of a symptom as generalized as this, particularly as neurotic anxiety is merely an exaggeration and prolongation of a universal and inevitable emotion. Sometimes, indeed, one suspects that the complaint of suffering from anxiety derives in part from the erroneous belief that a normal person would never be anxious, and that, therefore, to experience it even occasionally is abnormal. However, clinical and introspective analysis of the symptom 'anxiety', as complained of by anxiety-neurotics suggests that it is compounded of two elements; one, signal-anxiety, evoked by either external stress or by the sense that defences are failing, the other, emotions which arise as a response to stress or emerge as part of the return of the repressed which occurs when defences begin to fail. This second element is not, strictly speaking, a form of anxiety at all but some other emotion, the nature of which is not clearly apprehended by the patient but which he recognizes as distressing. It is sometimes fairly easy to sense that the patient who complains solely of anxiety is in fact on the verge of anger or tears or is in a state of sexual tension.

The fact that a person says he is anxious is not, of course, in itself evidence that he is, only that he thinks he is or wishes it to be believed that he is. Since psychiatrists and psycho-analysts tend to interpret all functional symptoms as either manifestations or derivatives of anxiety and since, further-more, as I mentioned in Chapter 1, they tend to use the word 'anxiety' to describe all kinds of mental distress or pain, it is not unusual to encounter patients who say that they are anxious but who display no signs of being so, at least in any definable sense of the term. I recently saw in consultation a man who claimed to have suffered persistently from anxiety for over ten years, and who gave a history of having had perhaps a hundred hours of psychotherapy during that time. As he appeared entirely at ease while telling his troubles to a perfect stranger, I enquired further and discovered that the fact on which his idea that he was anxious was based was persistent discomfort in his abdomen. This discomfort, which he and, apparently, his three psychotherapists, had all called anxiety, had never once kept him awake at night, put him off his food or prevented his driving a car or playing tennis. Now, although there must, of course, be something amiss with a man who has, or imagines he has, persistent abdominal pain, and although his various psychotherapists may have been right in supposing that anxiety lurked somewhere below the surface, this man did not suffer from anxiety. He believed he did and this provided him with a legitimate reason for seeking psychiatric help and reassurance about quite other matters.

Although it may seem odd that anyone should wish it to be thought that he suffered from anxiety, there are at least two reasons why this may happen. First, a tendency to feel anxious may be used as evidence of sensibility, of being a more tender plant than ordinary mortals. In sophisticated circles, the term *'angst'* may be preferred, since to suffer from *angst* is not only evidence of being sensitive but also of being attuned to the Age of Anxiety in which we allegedly live. Persons who suffer from *angst* are neither amused nor impressed by Dr Johnson's dictum that 'public affairs vex no man' and that they never caused anyone to sleep 'an hour less, nor eat an ounce less meat'. Secondly, a person may wish it to be thought that he suffers from anxiety in order to persuade others to protect him from situations which he wishes to avoid. This manoeuvre depends on the assumption that anxiety is not only an unpleasant experience but a harmful one, and that it is as cruel and dangerous to expect an anxious person to endure stress as it would be to expect a man with a broken leg to run a race. Persons who exploit the idea that anxiety is a symptom of illness habitually describe their anxiety as 'intolerable' or 'unbearable', but in fact rarely allow themselves to get into a position in which they might discover how much anxiety they can tolerate. Since the tendency to use defences begins in childhood, neurotics in general underestimate their capacity to tolerate anxiety; they assume without question that their ego is still as fragile as it was when the original defence-evoking traumata occurred.

In the previous paragraph I have been discussing hysterical manipulation of the idea of anxiety, not anxiety itself, and I am not suggesting that all neurotic anxiety is of this kind. On the contrary, chronic, persistent anxiety is a very real and distressing symptom and, since anxiety is a physiological state of heightened alertness, it causes its victims to live permanently at a level of tension which healthy persons only experience intermittently. As a result, patients with anxiety-neurosis suffer from physical symptoms of two kinds: those which are the physical accompaniment of anxiety, and those which are the effect of sustained stress.

In anxiety, as in fear, the body goes into a state of heightened activity. The heart beats faster, respiration is accelerated, the muscles are tensed and sight and hearing become more acute. The body is prepared for emergency action, but there is no appropriate action to take. As a result, the physical sensations of anxiety are themselves experienced as symptoms. Unlike a frightened person, who has no time to become aware of, or concerned with, the details of his bodily state, the anxious patient becomes acutely aware that his heart is pounding, that he is over-breathing, that he is tense, while his heightened visual and auditory acuity makes him irritable and literally 'over-sensitive'. These physical symptoms may indeed be taken as the cause and not the effect of the anxiety, and many patients who are in fact anxious complain in the first instance of suffering from palpitations, breathlessness or muscular pains. In former days cases of anxiety-neurosis were not infrequently diagnosed as suffering from heart-disease, a diagnosis which must have further increased their anxiety and which led to much unnecessary invalidism.

In addition to suffering from the physical manifestations of anxiety, patients with anxiety-neurosis are also liable to suffer from fatigue and exhaustion. The effort of maintaining for long periods of time a physiological state designed to deal with short-lived emergencies is in itself exhausting, an effect which is enhanced by the fact that anxiety is incompatible with sound sleep. Furthermore, the fact that neurotic anxiety, unlike fear and normal vigilance, has no appropriate avenues of discharge, means that the anxiety-neurotic expends energy inhibiting the urge to action which forms part of his anxiety. As a result, persons with anxiety-neurosis are liable to suffer from tension states which derive as much from the need to control anxiety as they do from the fact of experiencing it.

From a theoretical point of view, anxiety-neurosis can be regarded as a failure of the defensive techniques which I described in the last chapter, and they probably occur either *before* these have become established, as in the anxiety-states of childhood and adolescence, or *after* they have been undermined by some change in the patient's mode of life. Certainly, anxiety-neuroses seem often to develop after leaving home or school, after coming down from the university, after marrying, after the birth of a first child, after promotion from a subordinate to a responsible position at work or after retirement, i.e. after some change of circumstances which renders a familiar pattern of behaviour and defence inappropriate or inadequate. In psychotherapy it is often possible to demonstrate that a phase in which anxiety was the only symptom preceded the development of one of the other neuroses.

NEUROTIC DEPRESSION

I have already discussed neurotic depression in Chapter 3, where I described two different kinds of depression: melancholic depression, in which the patient feels guilt and remorse, and behaves as though he had committed some terrible crime, and a more general feeling of depressed vitality which occurs when inhibition is excessive. Both the latter and milder cases of the former may lead to a diagnosis of neurotic depression. This diagnosis resembles that of anxiety-neurosis in that it simply describes the patient's main symptom, while at the same time asserting that it is due neither to physical illness nor to psychosis. In the case of neurotic depression this latter qualification is of practical importance since depression is the main symptom of one of the functional psychoses, manic-depressive psychosis, in which there is an ever-present risk of suicide. According to Henderson and Gillespie's *Textbook of Psychiatry*, cases diagnosed as 'neurotic depression' are either hysterical or mild cases of manic-depressive psychosis. However, the emotions of anxiety, guilt and depression are, as I described in Chapter 3, so subtly inter-connected that the complaint of feeling depressed may occur in any of the neuroses.

OBSESSIONAL NEUROSIS

I have already discussed some features of obsessional neurosis in Chapter 3, where I described how internalization of strict, authoritarian parental figures leads to conflict between the superego and other parts of the self, and how this conflict leads to neurotic guilt and to the development of obsessional thoughts and rituals. I have also described in Chapter 5 the type of character which develops in persons who habitually use obsessional defences. Obsessional neurosis occurs typically in persons who have previously had obsessional personalities, though the correlation is not perfect. According to Pollitt (1960) thirty-four per cent of 115 cases of obsessional neurosis had had no obsessional character-traits before breakdown, while obsessional personalities are also liable to develop depression, which can be regarded as an intensification of the obsessional sense of guilt.

The symptoms of obsessional neurosis are of two kinds: compulsive or intrusive thoughts and images, and compulsive acts or rituals. Compulsive thoughts differ from normal thinking in that they are alien to the patient's conscious attitudes and values and are experienced by him as intruders and interrupters of his spontaneous flow of thoughts and feelings. Freud in his paper 'Notes upon a case of Obsessional Neurosis' (1909) described a young man who felt compelled to imagine rats gnawing at the anuses of his fiancée and father – this despite the fact that he had the greatest respect for his fiancée and that his revered father had been dead for some years. This example illustrates vividly most of the characteristic features of obsessional thoughts; they tend to be bizarre, absurd, distressing and coarse, usually in striking contrast to the patient's refined, orderly, logical and high-minded conscious personality. Other patients are obsessed by the thought that they may suddenly be impelled to perform some outrageous or grossly inappropriate action. I have already mentioned earlier the obsessional fear of being compelled to utter blasphemies in church. Another example of the same kind of phenomenon was provided by a young woman who found it almost unbearable to eat at the same table as her husband; she was tormented by the idea that she might find herself compelled to impale one of his fingers on her fork. This thought was not an expression of conscious hostility towards her husband, to whom she was devoted.

Other obsessional patients are obsessed by the thought that they may not have done what they know they in fact have done. Such patients have to check and re-check that they have in fact turned off the gas, locked up the house, or done their accounts correctly, despite the fact that they have a clear recollection of having performed the action correctly the first time. These obsessional doubts may on occasion become so severe and all-pervasive that they bring the patient's life to a standstill. It is characteristic of obsessional thoughts and doubts that they can fairly readily be interpreted as evidence of a greater degree of ambivalence than the patient has any inkling of. The obsessional thought either expresses some repressed impulse in disguised form or it represents an attempt to ward off the emergence of such an impulse. It would be a mistake, however, to think that the ambivalence is always directed towards the apparent object of the obsessional thought. The woman who compulsively imagined herself impaling her husband's finger on a fork was not ambivalent towards her husband as an individual in his own right but only as a representative of the general category, man, towards whom she was ambivalent.

Compulsive actions are usually in themselves trivial and derive their distressing quality from the fact that the patient nonetheless feels compelled to repeat them and becomes anxious if he fails to do so. They can conveniently be thought of as privately constructed superstitious rituals. Clothes, the objects on a table or mantelpiece, have to be laid out in a particular, usually symmetrical manner. Washing has to be done according to a particular routine and certain objects must either be avoided or touched whenever passed. The common childhood habit of having to avoid putting a foot on the cracks between paving stones is often cited as a typical obsessional action, although the majority of children who do this do not develop an obsessional neurosis in adult life. Other obsessionals develop counting compulsions; they have to count up to such-and-such a number before making a decision, they have to count the number of steps on every staircase they climb or the number of paces they take while going for a walk, or they have to avoid certain numbers and use numerical circumlocutions if the taboo number, which is not always thirteen, has to be used in a calculation. These acts have in common the fact that they are pointless, and are recognized by the patient as pointless, but are nonetheless felt to be necessary to ward off some unspecified evil – if they are not performed something dreadful will happen either to themselves or their parents, spouse or children, though what that something might be is usually not clearly formulated. Like superstitious acts they are attempts to ward off irrational fears by equally irrational actions and the logic underlying them is that of magic not of science or common sense. They can be regarded as perversions of the defensive technique of mastery which I described in Chapter 5; feeling threatened by forces within himself which he does not understand and which seem inexplicable in terms of the laws of reason, the obsessional responds in kind by developing an equally magical system of counter-magic.

PHOBIAS

I have already discussed phobias in Chapter 1 where I cited them as the simplest example of neurotic anxiety and listed the objects and situations which most commonly provoke phobic anxiety, while in Chapter 5 I gave an account of the phobic defence. I have also mentioned earlier in this chapter that some psychiatrists regard phobic symptoms as a manifestation of anxiety-neurosis while others think of them as obsessional. A phobia differs, however, from an anxiety-neurosis in that phobic anxiety is evoked by some specific object or situation whereas the anxiety in anxiety-neurosis is generalized and free-floating, while it differs from an obsessional neurosis in that the emphasis in the latter is on some specific, stated action which must be taken to avoid dread of something unspecified. Although neither the phobic nor the obsessional really knows what provokes his anxiety, the phobic thinks he knows what it is but feels incapable of mastering it, while the obsessional thinks he knows how to control it without knowing what it is. In other words, although phobia and obsessional neurosis resemble one another in that their symptoms are defences against the anxiety which is manifest in anxiety-neurosis, they differ in that one uses the defence of avoidance and the other that of control.

Anxiety and Neurosis

HYSTERIA

Anxiety-neurosis, obsessional neurosis and phobia are terms of fairly recent origin, the first two indeed having been originally introduced by Freud, and they are all diagnoses which simply describe the major symptom of the condition to which they refer. They are merely convenient descriptive labels and no one seriously pretends that they are anything more than this. With hysteria, however, things are very different. It is a medical concept which has been in use since the time of the Ancient Greeks and the idea still lingers on that it is a specific disease like typhoid fever or multiple sclerosis. It also differs from the other psychiatric diagnoses in carrying derogatory overtones; to describe someone as hysterical is to raise the possibility that he may be acting, malingering or being insincere. These two factors combine to make hysteria a highly unsatisfactory term and in 1952 the American Psychiatric Association eliminated it from their Standard Nomenclature of Diseases, replacing it by the term 'conversion-symptom'. It is still, however, included in the International Classification of Diseases 1955 (although in the extended form – 'hysterical reaction without mention of anxiety-reaction') which is the classification used by the National Health Service in this country.

However, the idea of hysteria dies hard and it is a diagnosis which still frequently appears on case-sheets. The nearest to a precise definition of hysteria that one is likely to reach is that it is a condition in which (*a*) the patient complains of physical symptoms which are nonetheless unaccompanied by any signs of organic disease, (*b*) the symptoms correspond to the patient's idea of how his body works and not to the actual facts of anatomy and physiology and (*c*) the patient is not anxious, resists the idea that his symptoms may be of psychological origin and reacts evasively to all attempts to discover whether he has psychological and personal problems.

Hysterical phenomena, such as paralysis of the arms or

legs, blindness and loss of voice, fits and fainting attacks, are, since Freud, described as conversion-symptoms, on the ground that they are due to the conversion of an idea into a physical symptom, as a result of which the patient ceases to be concerned with some distressing idea, memory, emotion or conflict and instead develops a physical disability for which he, or more usually she, can seek medical assistance. In the previous chapter I suggested that this process of conversion is a means by which patients who feel that they are unable to assert themselves and their rights straightforwardly are enabled to make use of the submissive role and the effect it has of disarming others, to claim the attention to which they basically feel that they are not entitled. It is remarkable that although psycho-analysis and psycho-pathology began with the study of hysteria, the mechanism by which hysterical conversion is effected remains entirely mysterious; and that it is not known why some people are able to use this defence while others are not. There seems, however, to be general agreement that hysteria is a psychological illness.

The process of conversion is responsible for the hostility which hysterics, despite Freud, still not infrequently encounter from both their relatives and their physicians. Both sense that the symptoms are not quite what they seem to be and that the patient is asking for something other than what is apparently being asked for, while the physician finds himself being asked to relieve a symptom which is only a caricature or simulacrum of the kinds of disability which he has been trained to treat. As a result, both feel that they are being put into a false position, that of being asked to help someone who cannot, or will not, tell them what is the matter, and tend to react with exasperation. Alternatively, hysterics lay themselves open to conscious or unconscious quackery from therapists who go along with their idea that they are physically ill. Hysterical patients who reach an analyst's couch almost always give a history of having had previous treatment from practitioners of various forms of fringe medicine such as osteopathy, acupuncture or Christian Science.

The position is further compounded by the fact that hysterical patients are usually women, while their physician is usually a man. As a result, the demand for attention and the dramatic, histrionic way in which the hysterical woman presents her symptoms leads to her physician feeling threatened by the pressure of the unspecified emotional demands that are being made upon him and which are, he often suspects, and often rightly, basically sexual in nature. Joseph Breuer, co-author of the *Studies on Hysteria*, which converted Freud from a neurologist into a psycho-analyst, retired from the scene when he appreciated to what an extent hysteria was a sexual disorder.

The idea that hysteria is a sexual disorder is implicit in its name, which derives from *hysteron*, the Greek word for the womb. Until the end of the eighteenth century, hysterical symptoms were commonly explained as being due to some disturbance of the uterus. According to one theory, the uterus is a mobile organ – some writers even considered it to be an animal – which could wander about the body, pressing on other organs and putting them out of action. According to another, hysteria was the result of sexual abstinence which led to 'suffocation of the womb' by the retained animal spirits which should have been released in sexual intercourse. These spirits or 'vapours' were also believed to pass out of the uterus into other organs, casting a blight upon them and causing paralyses, choking sensations and fits. With tedious regularity the literature describes hysteria as occurring more frequently in virgins and widows than in wives, and in ladies with moral reputations to maintain than in simple peasant and working girls. According to Ilza Veith, from whose *Hysteria: The History of a Disease* I have abstracted these pre-scientific and pre-analytical theories of hysteria, the incidence of hysteria has undergone a class-reversal in the present century; she asserts that it only occurs among 'the uneducated of the lower social strata' and attributes this to the dissemination of psycho-analytical ideas. Nonetheless, psycho-analysts in private practice are not unfamiliar with hysterical phenomena.

One of the major achievements of nineteenth-century medicine, and of Freud in particular, was to rescue patients with conversion-symptoms from this farrago of superstitious nonsense and from the ridiculous and often brutal forms of treatment to which it gave rise, and to make hysteria a legitimate subject for scientific investigation. The physiologists and neurologists demonstrated that the uterine theories of hysteria were fanciful, while Freud demonstrated that hysteria was a psychological and not a physiological disturbance. He also showed that hysterical symptoms could occur in men, although in this he had precursors. Sydenham, the seventeenth-century physician who is often described as the father of English medicine, recognized that men could have hysterical symptoms and got round the verbal objections to diagnosing hysteria in men by calling male hysterics hypochondriacs.

Although conversion-symptoms are the cardinal sign of hysteria, there are also a number of other conditions which are traditionally labelled hysterical. These include loss of memory (hysterical amnesia), pseudo-dementia, in which the patient behaves in a way which corresponds to his idea of how a defective or insane person would behave, sleep-walking, fugues, in which the patient wanders off no longer knowing where or who he is, and double or multiple personality, in which the patient switches from one personality to another like the fictitious Dr Jekyll and Mr Hyde, being oblivious while in one personality of the actions he performed while in the other.

These conditions resemble conversion-hysteria in demonstrating the existence of split-off, dissociated mental activity, of which the central personality is unconscious, and in conveying to others the uncanny feeling that the patient has been taken over by some force other than himself. Another of the pre-scientific theories of hysteria was that it was due to possession by demons. Sometimes the hysteric was held to be the involuntary victim of the demon who had possessed her, in which case attempts were made to exorcise her by the appropriate religious ceremony; sometimes she was held to be a willing collaborator with the devil, with whom she had had intercourse, and was regarded as a witch. Both Ilza Veith, whom I have already cited, and Zilboorg maintain that most of the witches who were persecuted with such brutality in the fifteenth and sixteenth centuries would nowadays be regarded as mentally ill and suffering from hysteria.

These other hysterical conditions also resemble conversion-hysteria in being amenable to interpretation in terms of motive. Indeed, most of them can be readily understood as means by which a person who feels helpless or trapped may nonetheless make a bid for freedom. Hysterical pseudo-dementia apparently only occurs in prisoners awaiting trial, hysterical loss of memory commonly follows some conflictual situation for which there is, or appears to be, no solution, while many of the cases of fugue described in the psychiatric textbooks concern boys at boarding-school and soldiers on active service.

SEXUAL SYMPTOMS IN NEUROSIS

Although this is a book about anxiety and the neuroses and not about sexual disorders, it should be mentioned that most neurotics complain of sexual difficulties and dissatisfactions of one kind or another. Since the neuroses are disturbances in personal relationships, anxiety and defences are likely to manifest themselves in the sphere of sexual behaviour and it would, indeed, be possible to use the schema I have adopted throughout this book to spell out in detail how anxiety itself, and the four defences against it, can interfere with spontaneous sexual enjoyment – how obsessional defences interfere with spontaneity, how schizoid defences tend to preclude full emotional participation, how phobic defences may produce impotence and frigidity, and how the hysterical, submissive defence leads in both sexes to a passivity and evasiveness which is not conducive to sexual happiness. There are, however, two objections or limitations to such a procedure.

Firstly, sexual behaviour involves two people and not one. Although it is entirely legitimate to regard an obsessional symptom or a phobia as a symptom of the person who complains of it, it is by no means easy to decide whether a sexual 'symptom' should be regarded as a manifestation of the intrinsic pathology of the partner who presents as a patient with it or as a reflection of the pathology of the other – or as evidence that there is something amiss with the relationship between them. If a man complains of impotence, it may be that he has a neurosis which would render him incapable under all circumstances and with any woman, but it may be that his wife has insurmountable inhibitions or that the relationship between them is one that precludes the possibility of sexual desire ever arising. It is not at all uncommon for men to accept their wife's charge that they are impotent, when in fact it is the wife who is off-putting, or for women to berate themselves for being frigid when their husbands have failed to awaken them; or for both parties to bandy accusations against one another when in fact the marriage is on a false basis.

Secondly, sexual behaviour is not solely a matter of functional capacity; it also raises questions of morality and sincerity which lie outside the scope of the clinical approach. Unhappily married people who seek to solve their marital problems by getting a psychiatrist to cure his 'impotence' or her 'frigidity' are usually, though not always, deceiving themselves; and if they are referred to a psychotherapist, they are likely to have to spend as much time reflecting upon the various falsities, grievances and disappointments which have accumulated during their marriage as they will discussing their sexual inhibitions.

PROGNOSIS

If this were a chapter in a medical textbook it would have to include some discussion of prognosis, i.e. of the likely duration of each neurosis and of the chances of recovery with and without treatment. Since, however, the various neuroses are not specific and mutually exclusive entities, and since individual patients may display symptoms of more than one of them simultaneously, and since, furthermore, it is not always possible to draw a hard and fast line between a neurosis and its corresponding defensive personality-type, psychiatric prognostication, at least of the neuroses, remains a most uncertain art. A number of generalizations are, however, possible. First, defensive patterns of behaviour are relatively constant. It is unusual for a person to switch from, say, a predominantly obsessional to a predominantly hysterical defensive adaptation. The reason for this is that defensive patterns are established in childhood; it is also possible that they may be influenced by constitutional, temperamental factors. Defensive patterns may, however, become more or less rigid with the passage of time, and over the years a person may grow more or less obsessional or hysterical. Secondly, defences and symptoms which depend on internalization and whose function is to prevent the re-emergence of repressed, unconscious forces are, without treatment, less likely to change than those which are responses to external stress. Depressive, obsessional, schizoid and phobic symptoms, which are highly complex psychopathological phenomena involving the use of internalization, projection and symbolization, are much less likely to disappear spontaneously than are anxiety-states or conversion-symptoms. These latter are, in part at least, responses to present environmental disturbances and are therefore likely to abate if external circumstances improve. Conversion-symptoms – though not the propensity to produce them – seem to be particularly dependent on the attitude of persons in the patient's environment. If they are taken both seriously and at their face value, and if they lead to the kind of invalidism which brings with it attention and power, they are likely to persist indefinitely; but if they fail either to impress or to infuriate, they are likely to vanish as suddenly as they came. I have more than once left a patient with paralysed legs on my couch in perfect confidence that when I returned half an hour later both the paralysis and the patient would have departed.

Chapter 7

Treatment of
the Neuroses

Although the neuroses are correctly described as psychological illnesses, in that their origins are to be sought in the
individual's history and in his emotional relationships, both
past and present, this does not mean that they are without
physical manifestations and effects. Indeed, as I have emphasized throughout this book, two of the most distressing and
central symptoms of the neuroses, anxiety and depression,
are not simply mental phenomena but physiological, or
rather psychophysiological, experiences of our whole being,
which only verbal conventions compel us to describe as
though they consist of two concurrent types of experience,
one mental and the other physical. In this anxiety and
depression resemble all other emotions, both pleasant and
unpleasant.

As a result, the neuroses, or at least some of the manifestations of neurosis, are amenable to alteration by physiological
means, and both anxiety and depression can be either increased
or decreased by physical agencies. In practice, of course, the
number of occasions on which anyone would want to increase
either depression or anxiety must be very few, but, since
they are in many respects antithetical states of mind and body,

over-dosage of sedatives and hypnotics which have been taken to reduce anxiety are liable to induce depression, while over-dosages of stimulants and anti-depressants may induce anxiety.

The physical aspects of anxiety and depression are, then, treatable by pharmacological means and drugs are undoubtedly the commonest form of treatment which neurotics receive. These drugs are of various kinds and include a large range of sedatives, hypnotics, tranquillizers, anti-depressants and stimulants, which it would be out of place to discuss in detail here.

Their popularity, however, does not derive entirely or even mainly from their actual effectiveness, but also from a number of adventitious factors, such as the fact that most doctors have neither the time nor the training to practise any form of psychotherapy, while many, perhaps most, neurotics prefer the idea of relieving their immediate distress with medicines to that of embarking on a voyage of self-exploration. The use of drugs is, indeed, often a defence, inasmuch as it enables patients to deny the extent and nature of their illness and doctors to keep their patients at a psychological distance. As Dr Balint's work at the Tavistock Clinic has shown, general practitioners who become alerted to the extent to which requests for medicines to relieve trivial physical symptoms are veiled, unconscious pleas for psychological help, often find themselves in a position to treat neuroses of which they would otherwise have remained oblivious. For this to happen, however, an initial resistance on the part of both doctor and patient has to be overcome.

Another factor contributing to the widespread use of drugs in the treatment of the neuroses is that medicines retain their magic, as is shown by the fact that placebos – drugs which are pharmacologically inert – will often, temporarily at least, relieve neurotic anxiety. Many neurotics, particularly those who use phobic and hysterical defences, are highly suggestible and the combined prestige of the medicine and of the doctor who prescribes it will often have a reassuring effect. The efficacy of drugs appears, indeed, to be influenced by fashion and, as Ian Oswald has pointed out in his recent book *Sleep*, sleeping pills nowadays fulfil the role that used to be played by the laxatives which a generation ago all God-fearing citizens took daily. 'The nightly barbiturate has replaced the morning brimstone and treacle.' In 1963 National Health Service general practitioners prescribed five hundred million sleeping pills, twice as many as they had ten years previously, though no one suggests that the incidence of insomnia has increased twofold or that the nation is better rested and more energetic – or less anxious and neurotic – than it used to be.

A recent article in *The Practitioner* by Kessel gives a vivid account of the extent to which general practitioners are called upon to treat neuroses and of the futility of most of their endeavours. I quote the Medical Correspondent of *The Times*'s admirable and amusing summary:

G.P. has no time to deal with Neuroses

'Optimal management of neurotic patients by their general practitioners is not possible under the National Health Service', says the assistant director of the Medical Research Council unit for research on the epidemiology of psychiatric illness, in today's issue of *The Practitioner*.

His logic is devastating. It has been estimated that in one year a general practitioner will be consulted for a neurotic illness by 8·9 per cent of all those adults registered with him. In a practice of 2,500 patients, including children, this means about 175 adults.

'Suppose five minutes a week were allotted to each of these patients, though this is surely a great underestimate of their needs. Allow a minute between consultations to write notes and usher in the next patient. The practitioner will be occupied for $17\frac{1}{2}$ hours a week, more than the equivalent of the whole of every working afternoon.' As is pointed out, it is clearly impossible for the practitioner to give so much of his time.

The position is further complicated by the fact that there is no agreed effective treatment and that 'it is becoming increasingly respectable to be diagnosed as suffering from neurosis'. Thus the number of people 'prepared to reveal its manifestations to their doctor, expecting to be treated, is likely to increase'.

On the tendency to treat these neurotic patients with drugs, the article says that 'it is doubtful if, had the millions of pounds worth of pills poured down the throats of neurotics consisted of nothing but starch, they would have been any less efficacious. Certainly they would have been much safer'.

Why then do doctors continue to prescribe so much? 'It is certainly not', it is categorically stated, 'that they are taken in by the blandishments of manufacturers'. It is for the simple reason that some treatment must be given and in present conditions this almost inevitably involves some form of drug.

'The biggest calamity that could beset general practitioners today,' it is claimed, 'would be the discovery of an effective but time-consuming method of treating neurosis', because they would feel bound to employ it and consequently would never get through the rest of their work. On the other hand, 'the biggest boon would be the production of a potent pill' – but of this there is no sign yet.

The article says the National Health Service is not equipped to provide adequate facilities for the treatment of neurosis. 'Perhaps therefore its managers ought to make it plain that the service cannot accept responsibility for this section of illness. At least the practitioner would not then have to labour under the sense that the blame is his.

'Yet, in practice, such a disclaimer by the N.H.S. would be impossible . . . so we have to struggle on, practising ineffectively. Until the theoretical understanding of how to treat neurosis is achieved, until there is considerably more money to spend within the N.H.S. the problem of how to manage the mass of neurotic patients known to their doctors cannot be satisfactorily solved.'

The one gleam of hope in this darkening scene is that a recent study in a Scottish border town indicates that most neurotics get better.

In addition to being of doubtful efficacy, the drugs which are used in the treatment of the neuroses also have a number of disadvantages.

Firstly, all drugs which reduce anxiety must, of necessity, also reduce vigilance. They therefore tend to reduce the efficiency with which the patient performs difficult or dangerous tasks and the speed with which he reacts to emergencies. In a recent 'information circular' issued by the Ministry of Aviation airmen are advised that 'fear is normal and provides a very effective alerting system. Tranquillizers and sedatives depress this alerting system and have been a contributory cause of fatal aircraft accidents.' (See *The Lancet*, 24 July 1965.) Although few of us are pilots, terrestrial activities also have their moments of danger requiring quick and intelligent responses, and the use of drugs which reduce vigilance is not without its risks, particularly as the usual justification for prescribing them is to enable patients to continue at work despite their neurosis.

Secondly, these drugs, even when they do relieve symptoms, do nothing to enlighten the patient as to their cause or meaning. Even if a patient does recover from a neurosis after a period of taking medicine, he is no wiser than he was before and, therefore, as likely to get into the same sort of state again. If it were not for the shortage of persons capable of giving psychotherapeutic help, this would be the major objection to the wholesale treatment of the neuroses by drugs. As it is, however, the use of drugs has at least the merit that it enables both doctors and patients to conform to the convention that some treatment is better than none, and that it is the patient's right and the doctor's duty to do something, even when the latter privately believes that he can do nothing effective. This last sentence will only sound cynical to those purists who believe that the doctor's role should be confined to administering therapies with a proved scientific basis and that he should eschew all actions which pander to the psychological need for benevolent gestures and reassuring, comforting rituals – and who forget that society has assigned the medical profession ceremonial as well as therapeutic functions.

It will already have become obvious that I consider psychotherapy to be the treatment of choice for the neuroses, but before discussing it, it is necessary to consider briefly a comparatively new form of treatment which is usually known as behaviour-therapy. This form of treatment has achieved a certain amount of prominence, largely because it has been used by Professor Eysenck as a stick with which to beat the psycho-analysts; this despite the fact that there exists a school of thought which holds that there is no real incompatibility between psycho-analytical theory and learning-theory, which provides behaviour-therapy with its theoretical basis. Both psycho-analysis and learning-theory assume that the neuroses are the effect of past experience on present behaviour, but while psycho-analysis formulates this effect in terms of such concepts as repressed memories and drives, learning-history does so in terms of faulty learning and conditioning. These different theoretical assumptions lead, however, to different therapeutic techniques, though behaviour-therapy resembles psycho-analysis in attacking neuroses through the mind not the body. Whereas psycho-analytical technique is designed – or rather was designed in the first instance – to enable repressed memories to be recovered, behaviour-therapy is designed to re-condition patients by altering the associations they have to whatever situations make them anxious or impel them to act abnormally.

The paradigm of behaviour-therapy was provided by J. B. Watson, the American psychologist, who first induced a phobic fear of white rats in an eleven-month-old orphan, Albert, by making a loud noise whenever Albert tried to play with the rats and then got his assistant, Mary Cover Jones, to cure the phobia by offering Albert a chocolate whenever he saw a white rat. This de-conditioning treatment of the experimentally-induced neurosis took, however, a certain time, since Albert at first took no notice of the chocolate, being simply intent on getting away from the rats. She therefore put the rats in the far corner of the room in which the experiment was being conducted and found that under those conditions Albert accepted the chocolate readily, although still casting a wary eye at the rodents. She then repeated the experiment, bringing the rats a little nearer each time, until Albert lost his fear of them and could again play happily with them. Although one cannot help hoping that the rats used in this epoch-making experiment were really white mice and wondering whether, if Albert had had a mother, she would have allowed him to be used as a subject, the scientific importance of this experiment is that it demonstrated that a phobia could be induced by conditioning and that it could be cured by de- or, rather, re-conditioning.

In the treatment of adult neuroses, more complex procedures are, of course, adopted. These include handling models or toys representing the phobic object, looking at photographs of it, talking about it, and being confronted with it while accompanied by the therapist.

Although behaviour-therapy began as a form of treatment for the phobias, it can also be used for some of the symptoms of the behaviour – disorders, such as fetishism, homosexuality or alcoholism, which can be treated by conditioning the patient to associate the fetish – or the male genitals, or alcohol – with unpleasant experiences in the hope that his perverse desires will be extinguished by disgust, pain or fear. This form of treatment is similar to one of the well-established treatments for alcoholism, aversion-therapy, in which the patient takes a drug which induces nausea whenever alcohol is taken.

Although behaviour-therapy is still in its early days, there are indications that it may recapitulate the early history of psycho-analysis. Psycho-analysis began as a form of treatment for specific symptoms, those of hysteria, and was at first regarded as an impersonal technique with a single aim, that of recovering repressed memories and abreacting the accompanying emotion, but in the event it turned out to be a treatment which relied largely on the personal relationship which developed between the patient and his physician and which involved much more than the recovery of a restricted number of specific repressed memories. Similarly, the journals are already reporting observations which suggest that behaviour-therapy is not simply an impersonal, mechanical technique for re-conditioning patients who have suffered from faulty learning, but that the personal relationship between therapist and patient which develops during de-conditioning sessions itself forms part of the therapeutic process. A recent article in *The British Journal of Medical Psychology* by A. J. Crisp entitled 'Transference in behaviour-therapy' describes the spontaneous development of trans-ference during the course of behaviour – therapy and quotes statistics suggesting that a positive transference enhances the efficacy of re-conditioning techniques. If this trend continues, the polemical attitude of some behaviour – therapists will begin to look a little silly.

However, psychotherapy remains the treatment of choice for the neuroses, although it must be admitted at once that there is no consensus of opinion about even such elementary points as which forms of psychotherapy are in general most efficient, or which forms of neurosis are most amenable to which kinds of psychotherapy.

There are many factors contributing to this unsatisfactory state of affairs, some of them intrinsic to the problems of psychological illness and therefore unavoidable, and others which are, perhaps, not altogether to the credit of those who practise psychotherapy. The former include the fact that the idea of doing psychotherapy at all is less than a hundred years old and that it is, therefore, not surprising that there should still be controversy about the basic principles of both theory and technique. Another is that psychological illnesses, the symptoms of which are largely subjective, are not readily amenable to either experimental or statistical investigation, the two tools by which the medical sciences usually establish basic principles and assess the effectiveness of forms of treat-ment derived from them.

Another unavoidable difficulty is that all theories about human nature encounter prejudice of both a positive and a negative kind. Freud's views on the pervasive influence of sexuality and Adler's on the primacy of the will to power encountered both prejudice *against* them from people who found these ideas repellent and *for* them from people who found them fascinating – both forms of prejudice which have, of course, nothing whatsoever to do with their truth.

We are here up against what may prove to be the limiting factor in the psychological sciences, the fact that there is something inherently paradoxical about the attempt to be objective about the subjective, or to study objects which are alive and like oneself by techniques derived from the study of objects which are inanimate and unlike oneself. Science has achieved its greatest successes in the study of the inanimate world and medicine in the treatment of those illnesses which can be regarded as mechanical disorders of individual organs or systems, but the neuroses are not only illnesses which people have but also disturbances in the way in which they function as persons. A physicist does not have to apply the laws of physics to his own personality, nor is a physician compelled to identify himself imaginatively with the workings of whatever bodily organ he is treating, but any psychotherapist worth his salt is compelled to come to an opinion as to what extent he is himself obsessional or hysterical – and to remain continuously alert to the effects that his personality may be having on his patients. He also has to take seriously the fact that any hypothesis to which his therapeutic experience may lead him, must also apply to himself.

It is not surprising, therefore, that in the field of psychotherapy some practitioners defend themselves against the anxiety which is aroused by operating in a territory with few familiar landmarks and where the principle of relativity holds sway by attaching themselves to some particular system of ideas, which is then held dogmatically – and to which they cling as tenaciously as a lost, anxious child clings literally to some familiar object. As a result, we have the emergence of rival schools of psychotherapy and psycho-analysis and the tendency of psycho-analytical organizations to undergo fission. In this country any prospective patient who decides that he wishes to have a Freudian psycho-analysis finds that he has to make a choice between three different sub-schools of thought – a state of affairs which is good for neither patients nor psycho-analysis.

The two previous paragraphs should not be taken as an argument in favour of either nihilism or scepticism, since there are, I believe, two ways of escape from the apparent *impasse* of relativism. One, which I have adopted throughout this book, is to base psychological theory on biology, while the other, to which I shall return later, is to regard the actual practice of psychotherapy as an exercise in communication. By interpreting, as I have, neurotic defences as elaborations and combinations of the responses of animals to situations of threat, I have been able to formulate a theory of neurosis which is independent of all fundamental assumptions about human nature, save that it is part of the evolutionary process, and without having to assert that *the* prime mover of human behaviour is sex, aggression, the will to power, or an inherent conflict between Eros and Thanatos, the life and death instincts. How many basic drives, instincts or inborn patterns of behaviour there are, is a problem of general biology, where it can be investigated without undue interference from either personal bias or speculative philosophizing. It is remarkable that none of the current psychodynamic theories, with their emphasis on sexual and aggressive drives, takes any account of behaviour in man which may be derived from the animal behaviour patterns of grooming and territoriality, despite the fact that these are instinctive activities as well authenticated as sex and aggression.

Nor have I found it necessary to argue that *the* origin of neurosis lies in Freud's Oedipus Complex, Melanie Klein's Depressive Position or any other specific psychological constellation. Although these terms refer to processes which can indeed be observed in analytical practice, they must, it seems to me, either be secondary phenomena which themselves require explanation or, alternatively, general human experiences which cannot, therefore, be used to explain those particular aberrations and restrictions of human development which we call neuroses. By conceiving of anxiety as a specific form of vigilance, neurotic anxiety as a special form of anxiety which arises as a by-product of the tendency of man to internalize his environment, and defences as responses which can be evoked by internal as well as external stress, I have endeavoured to formulate a general theory of neurosis which is compatible with a wide range of clinical assumptions about the pathogenic or traumatizing effects of particular experiences or phases of childhood.

The other avenue of escape from nihilism and scepticism is to regard the practice of psychotherapy as an exercise in communication. There are many kinds of psychotherapy, Freudian, Jungian, Adlerian, Kleinian, neo-Freudian, client-centred, non-directive, individual, group, supportive, interpretative – the number of possible qualifiers seems infinite – but they all have one thing in common: treatment consists of the establishment and maintenance of contact and communication between therapist and patient.

This is perhaps shown most clearly by the most modest form of psychotherapy, supportive psychotherapy, in which the therapist neither does, nor aims to do, more than listen, give moral support, sympathy and perhaps a little advice. Probably most of the psychotherapy given or practised is of this kind, and although it has none of the intellectual pretensions or glamour of its more sophisticated brethren, it has certainly helped many patients through emotional crises. Supportive therapy has rather cynically been described as 'the purchase of friendship', on the ground that it provides in the guise of a formal medical treatment the support and understanding that should be obtainable from spontaneously arising friendships. It is, indeed, a commentary on the extent to which modern society is not a community in any real sense of the term, that it should be necessary for highly trained personnel, such as doctors, psychologists and social workers,* to spend time on an activity which makes little or no use of their special skills. And although this is, it seems, unavoidable, it has at least two unfortunate consequences.

Firstly, it tends to seduce psychiatrists and psychologists away from doing research on the major mental illnesses. In the United States, where much more psychotherapy is practised than in England, William Schofield in his *Psychotherapy: the Purchase of Friendship* has sharply attacked the tendency of psychiatrists to offer treatment to persons who are unhappy or lost but who are in no definable sense ill. 'When prolonged psychotherapy is involved,' he says, 'the psychiatrist is perjuring medicine, the psychologist is failing what should be his basic commitment to research, and the social worker is being asocial.' He recommends the establishment of a new profession of counsellors, whose training would *not* include statistics, social pathology, psycho-analysis or anatomy.

The other unfortunate consequence of the pressure put on trained psychiatric personnel to provide sympathy is that it encourages those who have to do so to wrap up their modest but valuable activities in pretentious formulations. This process has been sympathetically described by Paul Halmos in *The Faith of the Counsellors*, where he argues that the counselling professions in fact give and believe in love but pretend to be scientific, and more acidly by Barbara Wootton and Edward Glover.

Supportive psychotherapy makes no claim to cure chronic

* Psychiatrists, clinical psychologists and psychiatric social workers are not the only persons who practise psychotherapy. If one defines psychotherapy as the treatment of persons in conflict by verbal communication, almost all members of the counselling professions are psychotherapists and much psychotherapy is in fact done by workers in Marriage Guidance and Family Planning Clinics, and by clergymen, probation officers, teachers and University tutors, though not all these would describe themselves as psychotherapists.

neuroses, which form the province of interpretative psycho-therapy. Here too the essential aim is communication between therapist and patient, though this is obscured by the fact that the therapist's most obvious activity is interpreting the patient's defences against communicating – an activity which is, of course, itself really a form of communication. Since neurotic patients are, by definition, either manifestly or latently anxious, they are ill-at-ease with their therapist and incapable of behaving spontaneously in his presence, and they therefore feel compelled to master their anxiety by the use of their habitual defences. The obsessional will try to control himself and his therapist, the schizoid will maintain an attitude of suspicious, superior aloofness, the phobic will either shrink away from contact with the therapist or, alternatively, seek protection by him, while the hysteric will make attempts to ingratiate himself or to evoke the therapist's sympathy. The therapist's task is, firstly, to point out to the patient what he is doing and, secondly, to demonstrate that these defensive manoeuvres are no longer necessary. The difficulties of psychotherapy – and the controversies between the different schools – arise in respect of this second phase of interpretative activity. After having ascertained that the patient is using a particular defence, the therapist has to decide what the patient is defending himself against. At this point the door is wide open to differences of opinion. Is the patient defending himself against his own impulses, or is he still compulsively using defences which were once necessary for external reasons? If the former, what is it about his impulses that makes him fearful of them? And how does the therapist set about helping the patient to discover that these are not as frightful or infantile as he fears? If the latter, what was the earlier situation which provoked a lasting defensive response, and how does the therapist prove to the patient that the past is no longer present?

In practice the answers to these questions are provided by the hints contained in what the patient says to the therapist, in the precise details of his symptomatology, in his gestures and slips of the tongue, in his dreams, and in the emotions he experiences in relation to the therapist. But since these hints are all indirect evidence from which inferences have to be drawn, both the theory of drawing inferences (e.g. dream-interpretation) and the particular inferences drawn can be subjects of controversy. Some therapists will be inclined to emphasize the inherent difficulties the human ego has in mastering its instinctual endowment, while others will emphasize the importance of early environmental conditions in alienating the individual from himself.

Fortunately, however, psychotherapy is a process involving two people, the patient as well as the therapist, and any theoretical bias the therapist may possess is likely to be at least partially corrected by the fact that the patient is an active participant in therapy, and one who is unlikely to be interested in the subtleties of theory or to continue treatment unless he feels that his own particular case is being understood. He therefore keeps the therapist down to earth and, since the actual process of psychotherapy is always concerned with particular and not general issues, progress is likely to depend on how well the two parties understand each other and how well they communicate within whatever frame of reference they happen to adopt. The theoretical differences between the various schools of psychotherapy seem to disrupt communication between therapist and therapist much more than that between therapist and patients.

Although severe, long-standing neuroses should ideally be treated by some kind of interpretative psychotherapy, the facilities for providing such treatment are inadequate, owing to the shortage of trained psychotherapists.* Nor is there any

* It is difficult to assess accurately how serious this shortage of trained psychotherapists really is, since no reliable data exist about the incidence of long-standing, complex neuroses of the kind which demand lengthy treatment. The classical Freudian view has always been that *all* neuroses are persistent disorders so deeply imbedded in the patient's personality and development that it is inconceivable they should remit spontaneously or that they

likelihood that the situation will improve within the foreseeable future – unless, of course, the 'potent pill' mentioned earlier proves after all not to be a mirage. There are several reasons for this.

Firstly, the training of psychotherapists is a long and expensive business, and in the absence of any consensus of opinion among psychotherapists as to how and what student therapists should be taught, public funds are hardly likely to become available in any quantity. As a result, the organizations providing an intensive training in psychotherapy, such as the British Psycho-Analytical Society and the Society of Analytical Psychologists, are likely to remain outside the National Health Service and the Universities and continue to be financed privately, mainly from the fees paid by the students themselves. One of the effects of the present situation is that the training courses available for students who wish to do intensive psychotherapy or psycho-analysis are of more use to doctors who intend to go into private practice than to those who wish to work within the National Health Service.

Secondly, a personal analysis seems to be an essential part of training – a point on which all schools seem to agree – and as this involves a commitment of up to eight hundred hours spread over four years, the number of students who can be trained by any one teacher is limited; and time spent on training students is time taken away from treating patients. As a result, the rate of production of psychotherapists is inevitably low.

will be influenced by anything short of a full analysis. Although the 'recent study on a Scottish border town' mentioned above (page 131), which indicates that most neurotics get better, strikes me as unduly optimistic, spontaneous recovery from even quite serious neuroses does sometimes occur, and, as I mention later, there is increasing evidence suggesting that suitably selected cases of severe neuroses can be helped by short-term psychotherapy. The theoretical conviction that this is impossible—and the therapeutic pessimism engendered by it – seems to derive from a failure to distinguish between character-neuroses and those which cause symptoms. Although the habitual, rigid modes of defence which distinguish character-neuroses are unlikely to dissolve spontaneously, only the psychologically sophisticated ever seek treatment solely on their account.

Thirdly, psychotherapy is itself a slow, time-consuming process. 'A full analysis' may last several years, and even brief psychotherapy of the kind recommended by D. H. Malan in his *A Study of Brief Psychotherapy* takes from ten to forty sessions. As a result, the number of patients any one therapist can treat is limited.

Attempts have, of course, been made to accelerate psychotherapy by combining it with hypnosis or drugs, or to increase the number of patients in treatment by group-therapy, in which the doctor treats five to ten patients at a time. These modifications of individual therapy, however, suffer from severe limitations, not the least of which is that, with some notable exceptions, the therapist himself is liable to regard them as regrettable, even if unavoidable, substitutes for the 'real thing'.

Fourthly, most of the pioneers of psychotherapy and psycho-analysis seem to have regarded their own forms of therapy as a panacea, by which everyone would benefit – except for those who were too ill to receive it. As a result, there has been very little systematic research into the problem of selecting patients for psychotherapy, and there remains a tendency to accept for treatment anyone who wishes to receive it, quite regardless of the nature or severity of their symptoms or of whether they are likely to require a short or a long analysis; and to insist on daily treatment sessions quite regardless of the diagnosis. One consequence of this is that psycho-analysts in particular are liable to spend their lives treating a very few patients for a very long time. D. H. Malan's book, which I mentioned above, represents a notable breakthrough, since it demonstrates that even severely ill patients may sometimes benefit from brief psychotherapy and gives specific criteria for deciding in advance which patients are likely to do so.*

* Dr Malan's book is based on research done at the Tavistock Clinic. It presents clinical and statistical material suggesting that patients with severe and long-standing neuroses may be given lasting help by brief psychotherapy,

These factors have conspired to produce the present paradoxical situation, in which psycho-analysis and psycho-therapy arouse great public interest, in which many psychiatric and analytical ideas have passed into general currency, and in which, as W. H. Auden has put it, Freud 'is no more a person now but a whole climate of opinion', but in which only a tiny proportion of the population has any direct experience of the therapeutic experience from which these ideas derive. It is therefore not surprising that many of the ideas which circulate as Freudian or psycho-analytical bear little or no relation to what Freud really said or analysts really do, or that many people think of psychiatry and psycho-analysis as exotic, esoteric theories and practices which lack any connection with medicine, biology or everyday life. This present book will, I hope, have done something to rectify this situation by showing that anxiety and the neuroses are phenomena which can be understood imaginatively as exaggerations of tendencies that are present in all of us and intellectually as manifestations of well-known biological principles.

---

provided that three conditions are fulfilled. Firstly, the therapist must adopt an active technique, selecting some particular problem as a focus for interpretation, instead of, as in classical psycho-analysis, interpreting whatever associations the patient happens to produce. Secondly, patients must be selected on the basis of the strength of their motivation for treatment and of their capacity to understand interpretations. And thirdly, the therapist must be prepared to enter into an 'objective emotional interaction' with the patient and interpret transference manifestations from the very beginning. Dr Malan's work assumes that the therapist is familiar with psycho-analytic concepts but that he should abandon three of the traditional rules of analytical technique: emotional detachment on the part of the therapist, caution in interpreting transference phenomena, and allowing the patient to decide the theme of each session.

Bibliography

Abraham, Karl, (1924) 'A Short Study of the Development of the Libido' in *Selected Papers on Psycho-Analysis* (London: Hogarth Press, 1949)

Alexander, Franz, *The Psychoanalysis of the Total Personality* (Nervous and Mental Disease Publishing Co., 1930)

Auden, W. H., 'In Memory of Sigmund Freud' in *Another Time* (London: Faber & Faber, 1940)

Balint, Michael, *The Doctor, His Patient and the Illness* (London: Pitman, 1957)

Barnett, S. A., 'The Biology of Aggression', *The Lancet* (10 October 1964)

Bleuler, Eugen, (1911) *Dementia Praecox* (International University Press, 1950)

Bowlby, John, 'Processes of Mourning', *International Journal of Psycho-Analysis*, vol. 42 (1961)
'Grief and Mourning in Infancy and Early Childhood', *Psychoanalytic Study of the Child*, vol. xv (1960)

Brown, Felix, 'Depression and Childhood Bereavement', *Journal of Mental Science*, vol. 107 (1961)

Butler, Samuel, (1903) *The Way of All Flesh* (London: Dent, 1954)
Erewhon (London: Dent, 1962)

Bibliography

Carstairs, G. M., 'Concepts of Insanity in Different Cultures', *The Listener* (30 July 1964)

Crisp, A. J., 'Transference in Behaviour-Therapy', *Brit. J. Med. Psych.*, vol. 39, pt 3 (1966)

Darwin, Charles, *The Expression of the Emotions in Man and Animals* (London: John Murray, 1872)

Durkheim, Emile, (1897) *Suicide* (London: Routledge & Kegan Paul, 1952)

Erikson, Erik H., *Young Man Luther* (London: Faber & Faber, 1959)

Evening Standard, 'Nightmares after Rail Crash', 10 March 1965

Eysenck, H. J., *Fact and Fiction in Psychology* (Harmondsworth: Penguin, 1965)

Fairbairn, W. R. D., 'A Revised Psychopathology of the Psychoses and Psychoneuroses' in *Psychoanalytic Studies of the Personality* (London: Tavistock, 1952)

Freud, Anna, *The Ego and the Mechanisms of Defence* (London: Hogarth Press, 1937)

Freud, S., (1909) 'Notes upon a Case of Obsessional Neurosis' in *The Psychological Works of Sigmund Freud*, standard edition, vol. x (London: Hogarth Press, 1955)
(1911) 'Psycho-Analytic Notes on an Autobiographical Account of a Case of Paranoia (Dementia Paranoides)', ibid. vol. xii
(1907) 'Obsessive Actions and Religious Practices', ibid. vol. ix (1959)
(1917) 'Mourning and Melancholia', ibid. vol. xiv (1957)
(1926) 'Inhibitions, Symptoms and Anxiety', ibid. vol. xx (1959)
(1940) 'An Outline of Psycho-Analysis', ibid, vol. xxiii (1964)
(1905) 'Jokes and their Relation to the Unconscious', ibid. vol. viii (1960)
'The Psychopathology of Everyday Life', ibid. vol. xi (1960)

with Breuer, J., (1893–5) 'Studies on Hysteria', ibid. vol. II (1955)

Glover, Edward, *The Roots of Crime* (London: Imago, 1960)

Gorer, Geoffrey, *Death, Grief and Mourning in Contemporary Britain* (London: Cresset Press, 1965)
'Psycho-Analysis in the World' in *Psycho-Analysis Observed*, ed. Charles Rycroft (London: Constable, 1966)

Gosse, Edmund, (1907) *Father and Son* (London: Heinemann, 1964)

Greenson, Ralph, (1949) 'The Psychology of Apathy', *Psychoanalytic Quarterly*, vol. XVIII

Halmos, Paul, *The Faith of the Counsellors* (London: Constable, 1965)

Hartmann, Heinz, (1939) *Ego Psychology and the Problem of Adaptation* (London: Imago, 1958)

Henderson and Gillespie, *Textbook of Psychiatry*, 9th edition (Oxford: O.U.P., 1962)

Kardiner, Abraham, 'The Neuroses of War' in *Contemporary Psychopathology*, ed. S. S. Tomkins (Cambridge, Mass: Harvard University Press, 1947)

Kessel, Neil, 'The Neurotic in General Practice', *The Practitioner*, vol. 194, p. 636 (1 May 1965)

Klein, Melanie, 'Notes on Some Schizoid Mechanisms' in *Developments in Psycho-Analysis* by M. Klein *et al.* (London: Hogarth Press, 1952)

Kubie, Lawrence, S., *Neurotic Distortion of the Creative Process* (Lawrence, Kansas: University of Kansas Press, 1958)

Laing, R. D. and Esterson, A., *Sanity, Madness and the Family*, vol. I (London: Tavistock, 1964)

Lambo, Professor T., 'Mental Health and Psychiatry in Nigeria', paper read to medical section of British Psychological Society, 29 September 1965

Lancet, 'In the Pink' (24 July 1965)

Leopardi, Giacomo, *Poems from Giacomo Leopardi* translated and introduced by John Heath-Stubbs (London: John Lehmann, 1946)

Bibliography

Liddell, H. S., *Emotional Hazards in Animals and Man* (Springfield, Illinois: Charles C. Thomas, 1956)
'The Role of Vigilance in the Development of Animal Neurosis' in *Anxiety*, ed. Paul Hoch and Joseph Zubin (New York: Hafner, 1950)

Lynd, Helen Merell, *On Shame and the Search for Identity* (London: Routledge & Kegan Paul, 1958)

McDougall, William, (1908) *An Introduction to Social Psychology* (London: Methuen, 22nd edition, 1931)

Malan, D. H., *A Study of Brief Psychotherapy* (London: Tavistock, 1962)

Mohr, J. W., Turner, R. E. and Jerry, M. R., *Pedophilia and Exhibitionism* (Toronto: Toronto University Press, 1964)

Oraison, Marc, 'The Psychoanalyst and the Confessor' in *Problems in Psychoanalysis* (London: Burns & Oates, 1963)

Oswald, Ian, *Sleep* (Harmondsworth: Penguin, 1966)

Pavlov, I. P., *Conditional Reflexes* (Oxford: O.U.P., 1927)

Pollitt, J. D., 'Natural History Studies in Mental Illness: A Discussion based on a Pilot Study of Obsessional States', *Journal of Mental Science*, vol. 106, p. 93 (1960)

Riesman, David, *The Lonely Crowd* (New Haven, Conn: Yale University Press, 1950)

Rycroft, Charles, 'Beyond the Reality Principle', *International Journal of Psycho-Analysis*, vol. XLIII (1962) and *Imagination and Reality* (London: Hogarth Press, 1968)
'Two Notes on Idealization, Illusion and Disillusion', *International Journal of Psycho-Analysis*, vol. XXXVI (1955) and *Imagination and Reality* (London: Hogarth Press, 1968)

Sartre, Jean-Paul, *Being and Nothingness: An Essay on Phenomenological Ontology*, translated by Hazel E. Barnes (New York: Philosophical Library, 1956)
Words, translated by Irene Clephann (London: Hamish Hamilton, 1964)

Schofield, William, *Psychotherapy: The Purchase of Friendship* (Englewood Cliffs, N.J.: Prentice-Hall, 1964)

Sherrington, Sir Charles, *The Brain and its Mechanism* (Cambridge: C.U.P., 1933)

Spinoza, Benedict, 'The Origin and Nature of the Emotions' in *Spinoza's Ethics* (London: Dent, Everyman Edition, 1960)

Tausk, Viktor, (1919) 'On the Origin of the Influencing Machine in Schizophrenia', *Psychoanalytic Quarterly*, 2 (1933)

Thomson, James, (1874) *The City of Dreadful Night* (Thinker's Library, 1932)

Times Medical Correspondent, 'G.P. has no time to deal with Neuroses', *The Times* (1 May 1965)

Tinbergen, N., *The Study of Instinct* (Oxford: O.U.P., 1951)

Veit, Ilza, *Hysteria: The History of a Disease* (Chicago, Illinois: University of Chicago, 1965)

Whitehorn, J. C., 'Physiological Changes in Emotional States', Research Publication Archives of Nervous and Mental Disease, vol. 19

Winnicott, D. W., *Collected Papers* (London: Tavistock, 1958)

Wolfenstein, Martha, *Disaster* (Glencoe, Illinois: Glencoe Press, 1957)

Wootton, Barbara, *Social Science and Social Pathology* (London: Allen & Unwin, 1958)

Zilboorg, Gregory, *History of Medical Psychology* (New York: Norton, 1941)

Index

Acts, compulsive, 117, 118
Adler, A., 136
Adolescent guilt, 43
Adrenal cortical secretion, 75
Aggression, suppressed, 74, 87–8
Agoraphobia, 64, 81, 84
Alcoholism, 103–4, 105, 134
Alertness (*see also* Vigilance)
   and anxiety, 4–7
Alexander, Franz, 105
Alienation, 60n.
Alloplastic maladaptation, 105
Amnesia, 60
   hysterical, 123, 124
Anaesthesia of the hands, 57
Analysis, in training psycho-
   therapists, 142–3
Angst, 18, 113
Animals, analogies to defence
   mechanisms, 74
Anomie, and neurosis, 106–8
Anti-depressant, 129
Anxiety
   automatic, 17
   and apprehensiveness, 1–3
   and alertness, 4–7
   alcohol and, 66
   castration, 10, 29

   and concern, 3–4
   of conscience, 73
   as a defence, 113–14
   definition, 5, 12, 16–17
   and efficiency, 14
   endurance of, 114
   enjoyment of, 8–9
   Freud's theory of, 9–10
   and fright, 18–20
   and the future, 7–9
   guilt and depression in, 36–54
   hope and, 8
   hysterical use of, 113–14
   imaginary, 112–13
   and inhibition, 59–60
   intellectual, 15
   instinctual, 73
   justifiable, 4
   libidinization of, 9
   meaning, 1
   necessity for, 6–7
   neurotic, xi–xii, 7, 9, 76
   objective, 73
   over-, 4
   primary, 9–10, 17
   separation, 10, 13–15
   shame and guilt in, 53
   and shock, 20–26

Index

Index

Index

Index

More about Penguins and Pelicans

A Pelican Original

The Psychology of Moral Behaviour

Derek Wright

It is by no means true that a sheltered 'moral'
upbringing, with lots of early nights and Sunday
school, produce the most honest, guilt-free people,
neither is altrusim the most helpful of qualities.

In *The Psychology of Moral Behaviour* Derek Wright of the
Department of Psychology at the University of Leicester
introduces the reader to the psychological study of
moral behaviour, and in particular to the empirical
approach within it. The author takes various theoretical
perspectives and examines the following subjects in
the light of them:

*Why some people find it easier to resist temptation than
others, and the psychological effects of doing something
wrong; what kinds of adult behaviour induce what kinds of
behaviour in children; delinquency; altruism; moral insight
and ideology; different types of character; religion; education
and morality.*

The author emphasizes the difficulty of discussing this
subject without being biased by personal beliefs, e.g.
Western moral ideas, and sets out to do so along the
strictest scientific lines.